5/23/13

For: Liza
and
Arnie

BLACK FLY STEW

Wild Maine Recipes

KATE KRUKOWSKI GOODING

Northern Solstice Publishing, LLC

Sophie and Sage, enjoying "The Way Life Should Be."

All cooking in this book refers to Fahrenheit scale.
The use of a trade name does imply endorsement
by the product manufacturer.

Black Fly Stew: Wild Maine Recipes
by Kate Krukowski Gooding

Editor:
Don Gooding

Artwork:
Cover art by Russell D'Alessio
Cover and book design by KAT Design, LLC
Art and photography (contact information, see Resources):
R. Scott Baltz
Gail Cleveland
Tom Curry
Kate Krukowski Gooding
Chris Krukowski
Marion Smith
Kat Stuart
Judy Taylor

ISBN 978-1-60402-047-2

This book is dedicated to my husband,

Don – my best friend, soulmate and

partner in life, with whom I share it all.

What a wonderful place to be!

PREFACE

I don't use real black flies in my cooking, but we do seem to eat a lot of them (no, wait, it's the other way around!) during black fly season here in Maine. The little bugs are part of Maine culture, and they crashed our June 2000 wedding in more ways than one.

Best man and best friend Jay Borden had given the "toast to the bride and groom" ahead of schedule (was it the champagne?), so he had to come up with another little speech for the originally planned toast. Jay and Ed Mitchell are well-known in our circle for their creative "Top Ten" lists. As they sat there swatting Maine's unofficial bird and thought about my inclination to "cook anything," they devised the "Number One Thing Heard at Don and Kate's Wedding" - "I heard Kate has a great recipe for Black Fly Stew!"

I loved the concept! We all laughed at the visual, but I packed the idea away for later. When this eclectic and wild collection of recipes began to take shape six years later, Black Fly Stew was the only way to describe the unexpected pleasures that spring from the wilds of Maine and a vivid imagination.

So here it is - the surprising result of a wedding toast! I hope you will immerse yourself in this cookbook and use it to create one of life's enjoyments - a meal remembered.

ACKNOWLEDGEMENTS

Thank you to the many testers of my first cookbook. You are an invaluable part of this process: Arlene Achey, Deborah Barlock, Lucille Bruce-Pedersen, Ashley Campbell, Howard Castonguay, Patty Puiia Cobb, Maggie Crawford, Linda D'Alessio, Don Gooding, Julia Gooding, Linda Hall, Jennie Hare, Jean Hazelton, Deborah Kallman, Dan Kennedy, Karen Kettlety, Kathy Mavrokas, Betty Mitchell, Beth Moody, Jennifer Munyer, Tobi Nichols, Roxanne Noddin, Kyle Pedersen, Allison Ponce, Dr. Kathleen Prunier, DVM, Diane Sammer, Deke Sharon, Cindy Smith, Anne Abbe Smith, and Kat Stuart.

Thank you to my many game meat, seafood and specialty food contributors: Dwayne Achey, Kelvin Achey, Bob Bowen *(Sunny Acres Farm)*, Jason Chapman, Michael Coyne *(MC Construction)* Tommy Giroux, Jr., Joe Hardison, Bob Hawkins *(Cold River Vodka)*, Mark Hodgdon, Wayne Hodgdon *(Lobsterman)*, Pesko Ivanov *(Bar Harbor Cellars)*, Chris Krukowski *(Maine Guide Service)*, Ron Musetti, Michael Musetti *(MCM Electric)*, Patty Penzey Erd *(The Spice Company)*, David Smith *(MDI Shellfish)*, Andrew Smith *(Mineral Springs Mushrooms)*, Kat Stuart *(KAT Design, LLC)*, and Tim Ziter *(Sweet Energy)*.

Special thanks to my mom, Constance Hall Krukowski, who guided me through the kitchen (OK, I may have forced her a little) at a very young age.

Last of all but not least, my appreciation goes to the talented artists whose work is represented in this cookbook; wine aficionados Don Gooding and Scott Worcester; chef and surrogate mother, Barbara Rogers Jolovitz; the cowgirls (you know who you are); and to my friend and graphics designer, Kat Stuart, whose talent and patience translated my ideas into this beautiful cookbook.

Contents

Artwork by Russell D'Alessio

Sides

Maple Walnut Granola
Goji Berry Granola
Raisin Bran Muffins
Fresh Salsa Chips
Asparagus Salsa
Wicked Island Princess Salsa
Downeast Cocktail Sauce
Eggplant Caviar
Kalamata Tapanade and Garlic Crostini
Roasted Red Pepper Hummus
Roasted Red Pepper Pesto Roll
Herbed Boursin Cheese
Roasted Veggie Tapanade
Smoked Salmon Cheese Ball
Vietnamese Spring Rolls with Peanut Sauce
Sun-Dried Tomato Split Pea Dip
Winter Solstice Paté
Hearty Hunter Biscuits
Honey-Graham Dinner Rolls
Whole Wheat and Rosemary Foccacia
Jasmine-Ginger Rice
Maine Maple Beans
Bread and Butter Pickles
Maple-Ginger Roasted Pecans
Fresh Basil Pesto
Kate's Spicy Mango Paste
Zucchini Relish

1

Artwork by Russell D'Alessio

Maple Walnut Granola

*The wonderful taste of local Maine maple syrup makes the
difference in this granola.*

5	cups old fashioned oatmeal
1	cup shredded, toasted coconut
1	cup pumpkin seeds
½	cup unsalted sesame seeds
1	cup dried cranberries
1	cup sunflower seeds
½	cup dried apples, chopped
1½	cups walnuts, chopped
1	teaspoon cinnamon, ground
½	teaspoon nutmeg, ground
¼	teaspoon mace
2	cups Maine maple syrup
¼	cup canola oil
¼	cup roasted walnut oil *(or use all canola oil)*
1	tablespoon vanilla

PREHEAT oven to 300°F.

COMBINE all dry ingredients in a large bowl. Combine all wet
ingredients in a second bowl and mix with dry ingredients until
coated. Spread ½ inch thick on oiled cookie pans, with sides. Bake
30 minutes on middle shelf, stirring every 10 minutes. Store in
airtight container.

Goji Berry Granola

5	cups old fashioned oatmeal
1	cup grapenut like cereal
1	cup shredded, toasted coconut
1	cup dried Goji berries*
1	cup sunflower seeds
1	cup pumpkin seeds
½	cup unsalted sesame seeds
1	cup dried apples, chopped
1	cup pecans, chopped
½	cup walnuts, chopped
1	teaspoon cinnamon, ground
½	teaspoon nutmeg, ground
¼	teaspoon allspice
2	cups Maine maple syrup
¼	cup canola oil
¼	cup roasted walnut oil (or use all canola oil)
1	tablespoon vanilla

PREHEAT oven to 300°F.

COMBINE all dry ingredients in a large bowl. Combine all wet ingredients in a second bowl and mix with dry ingredients until coated. Spread ½ inch thick on oiled cookie pans, with sides. Bake 30 minutes on middle shelf, stirring every 10 minutes. Store in airtight container.

COOK'S NOTE: For less crunchy granola, omit the grapenut like cereal

Goji berries have been used in Tibetan medicine for thousands of years. They're used to lower cholesterol, lower blood pressure and cleanse the blood.

Raisin Bran Muffins

If you like lots of raisins, add the optional cup of raisins in the list.

1¼   cups whole milk
1   cup raisin bran cereal
1½   cups flour
1   tablespoon baking powder
½   teaspoon salt
⅓   cup sugar
1   teaspoon ground cinnamon
½   teaspoon ground nutmeg
¼   teaspoon ground cloves
¼   teaspoon mace
½   cup butter, softened
¼   cup light molasses
1   large egg
1   cup raisins *(optional)*

PREHEAT oven to 400°F. Spray regular sized muffin tins with non-stick spray.

COMBINE the bran and milk; stir to moisten bran and let stand 10 minutes. Combine dry ingredients. Melt butter. Remove from heat and stir in molasses. Beat in egg. Add butter mixture to soaked bran and mix well. Add to dry ingredients and beat well. Stir in raisins.

SPOON into 12 muffin cups and bake 15 to 20 minutes or until a toothpick inserted in center comes out clean.

Fresh Salsa Chips

Tortilla wraps
Salsa Seasoning *(homemade recipe below)*
Non-fat cooking spray

CUT tortilla shells in different shapes, large enough for dipping. Spray with cooking spray and sprinkle with homemade salsa seasoning.

BAKE 375°F for 5 minutes or until crisp. Cool. Serve with salsa.

Salsa Seasoning

- 1 tablespoon sugar
- 2 tablespoons Ancho chili pepper powder
- 1 tablespoon garlic powder
- 1 tablespoon onion powder
- 1 tablespoon roasted, ground cumin
- 1 tablespoon mulatto chili pepper, ground
- 1 small, dried habanero *(optional for heat)*

GRIND all ingredients separately before combining together. Store in glass container.

COOK'S NOTE: To adjust heat on this fresh seasoning, start by omitting the habanero pepper and add ¼ piece at a time, and so on until you reach your desired heat level.

Asparagus Salsa

We started an asparagus bed in 2002; you cannot cut asparagus
until the third year, it takes two good years to root.
The harvest is worth the wait.

1	14-ounce can diced tomatoes
1 ½	cups asparagus cut 1" chunks
½	cup yellow onion, chopped
1	jalapeño, stemmed and chopped
1	tablespoon garlic, minced
½	teaspoon sea salt
2	tablespoons fresh lime juice
1	tablespoon Salsa Seasoning *(recipe p. 5)*
½	cup fresh cilantro, chopped

6

COMBINE all ingredients in food processor. Pulse just until blended. Keep that chunky, salsa look.

REFRIGERATE up to two weeks. Serve with fresh salsa chips. *(recipe p. 5)*

Wicked Island Princess Salsa

My favorite thing about this salsa is I harvest most of these
vegetables out of the garden around the same time.
The fresh taste is amazing.

5	very large beefsteak size tomatoes *(I grow Moskovich)*
½	cup finely chopped yellow onion

⅓ cup fresh orange juice
1 scotch bonnet pepper, coarsely chopped
1 ½ tablespoons lime juice
2 ounces tomato paste *(optional, for thicker salsa)*
1 ½ teaspoons salt
1 cup finely diced seedless cucumber
1 cup jicama root, shredded
½ cup chopped cilantro
3 tablespoons finely chopped spearmint

TRIM and half tomatoes. Gently squeeze out and discard seeds and juice and chop.

COMBINE first six ingredients in food processor, blend until smooth. Transfer to bowl and add the rest of the ingredients. Chill before serving.

COOK'S NOTE: I shred the jicama with a cheese grater, making long strands for the salsa. I love the presentation.

Downeast Cocktail Sauce

I make this sauce for the Layered Shrimp Dip (recipe p. 81).
I love the extra kick of the fresh horseradish.

1 ½ cups store bought cocktail sauce
1 tablespoon fresh horseradish
1 teaspoon Worcestershire sauce
1 teaspoon freshly squeezed lemon juice

MIX and refrigerate until use.

Eggplant Caviar

This is one recipe I've been making since my first
Winter Solstice Party in 1989.

1	medium-large eggplant
½	cup roasted walnuts, chopped
¼	cup minced red onion
1	tablespoon minced flat leaf parsley
½	teaspoon chopped chili
½	teaspoon chipotle peppers, chopped
½	teaspoon sea salt
3	garlic cloves, minced
⅛	teaspoon herbed peppers
½	teaspoon walnut oil
1	tablespoon olive oil
1	tablespoon Meyer fresh lemon juice

PRICK EGGPLANT in several places with fork or knife. Microwave on high 10 minutes, uncovered.

HOMEMADE roasted walnuts: In dry, cast iron frying pan slowly roast nuts until fragrance is released, about 7 minutes on medium heat. Stir a couple times to turn nuts over.

SCRAPE cooked eggplant from the flesh. Chop in wooden bowl.

ADD roasted walnuts, onions, parsley, peppers, garlic, salt and pepper. Slowly beat in oil and lemon juice. Cover loosely. Let stand at room temperature several hours before serving.

SERVE with white crackers or sliced baguette.

Kalamata Tapanade and Garlic Crostini

I had never been a fan of olives until I went to Agidir, Africa. Anne and I discovered an old olive oil mill with a donkey pulling a stone, crushing the olives. It was the best olive oil I have ever tasted. The only way I can taste anything close is to eat great olives, so I do!

1   cup Kalamata olives, pitted and chopped
1   can anchovy fillets, rinsed and chopped
¼   cup packed fresh flat-leaf parsley leaves, chopped
1   tablespoon red onion, minced
⅓   cup extra virgin olive oil
1   baguette, cut in 1½ inch slices on an angle
1   garlic clove, crushed
    extra virgin olive oil for drizzling

IN A FOOD PROCESSOR pulse olives, anchovies, parsley and onion with oil until coarsely chopped.

TOAST bread under broiler. Rub toast with crushed garlic. Top with tapanade and drizzle with extra-virgin olive oil.

COOK'S NOTE: I like to add a little feta cheese for a change.

Roasted Red Pepper Hummus

This is quick, easy to make and a crowd pleaser.

2 cups canned chickpeas, drained and rinsed
1 ½ cups canned roasted red pepper, drained, patted dry and chopped
4 garlic cloves
1 teaspoon Chris's Hot Sauce *(recipe p. 183)*
¼ teaspoon liquid smoke
2 tablespoons lemon juice
1 tablespoon honey
2 tablespoons tahini
½ cup olive oil
 salt and pepper to taste

FOOD PROCESS chickpeas, garlic, hot sauce, lemon juice, honey and tahini in the bowl of a food processor and process until smooth. With the machine running, slowly add the olive oil until emulsified. Serve with toasted baguette slices, crackers or fresh vegetables.

Roasted Red Pepper Pesto Roll

1 cup fresh basil leaves
¼ cup grated Parmesan cheese
¼ cup roasted pine nuts

3 large garlic cloves
¼ cup Portuguese olive oil
8 ounces goat cheese
3 roasted red peppers, drained from jar and blotted dry
1 baguette, sliced diagonally
  olive oil for brushing

COMBINE basil, cheese, pine nuts and garlic in food processor, pulse until combined but not pureed. On low, add olive oil until mixed well.

CUT roasted red pepper in half, vertically, and roll out into rectangle. Cut vertically in half again. Then spoon a thin mixture of pesto onto peppers and dot with goat cheese. Roll and slice.

TOAST baguette and brush with olive oil. Top with roasted pepper pesto roll.

Herbed Boursin Cheese Spread

1 package *(8 ounces)* cream cheese, softened
2 cloves garlic, minced
1 tablespoon fresh parsley, minced
1 tablespoon fresh minced chives
⅛ teaspoon cayenne pepper, to taste
⅛ teaspoon coarsely ground black pepper

COMBINE all ingredients in a bowl. Mix with the back of a large spoon until combined. Best served after spread has chilled in refrigerator for 4 hours, for flavors to meld.

Roasted Veggie Tapanade

A little curry in this dish adds to the roasted flavors.

2   tablespoons olive oil
2   red onions, chopped
2   Roma tomatoes, chopped
4   garlic cloves, chopped
1   cup yellow peppers
2   teaspoons spicy powdered curry *(Maharajah*)*
2   tablespoons minced flat parsley
    salt to taste
1   baguette, sliced diagonally

PREHEAT oven to 450°F.

RUB 12 inch roasting pan with olive oil. Add onions, tomatoes, peppers, garlic cloves and peppers. Bake for 45 minutes. Turn every 15 minutes.

PULSE roasted vegetables in food processor. Add curry, parsley, and salt and pulse until blended.

TOAST baguette, drizzle a little olive oil and sprinkle sea salt before you put the tapanade on, which adds another breadth of flavor.

* Available from The Spice House, see Resources.

Smoked Salmon Cheese Ball

Keep a can of salmon in the larder for this easy,
crowd pleasing appetizer!

8	ounces canned pink salmon, flaked with no bones
8	ounces cream cheese, room temperature
1 ¼	cups shredded white cheddar cheese
2	tablespoons minced yellow onion
1	tablespoon dried parsley
1	tablespoon lemon juice
1	teaspoon liquid smoke
½	teaspoon celery seed, ground fine
½	teaspoon garlic powder
½	cup finely chopped pecans or pistachios

COMBINE all ingredients except nuts. Shape into ball or log.
Chill. Roll in nuts before serving.

Vietnamese Spring Rolls with Peanut Sauce

Spring Roll

6	tablespoons canola oil
½	pound shrimp *(large, raw, shelled and deveined)*
2	shallots, thinly sliced
2	garlic cloves, minced
8	ounces jicama, cut into 2" x ¹/₉" matchsticks*
4	ounces carrots, 2 x/ matchsticks
3	tablespoons Mirin *(rice wine)* or sake
½	cup chicken stock
1	tablespoon fish sauce
1	tablespoon sesame oil
15	5-inch rice paper rounds
½	head red lettuce torn into 4" pieces
15	large basil leaves

14

TOSS shrimp in 2 tablespoons of canola oil and a dash of salt.

IN LARGE SKILLET HEAT 3 tablespoons of canola oil at medium-high and add shrimp. Cook until pink, about 1 minute. Set aside to cool in medium bowl. Add remaining 2 tablespoons canola oil to skillet. Add garlic and shallots and cook about 1 minute. Add carrots and jicama and cook until tender, about 4 minutes. Add wine, cook 3 minutes to reduce slightly. Add stock, fish sauce and sesame oil and bring to a boil. Reduce heat, cook 4 minutes longer. Drain vegetables and toss with shrimp and cool.

*COOK'S NOTE: A good substitute for jicama is water chestnuts

Peanut Sauce

½   cup cooked brown rice *(or jasmine)*
1   tablespoon light miso
¼   cup dry roasted salted peanuts
1   jalapeño, seeded and chopped
2   garlic cloves, chopped
1   tablespoon ketchup
1   tablespoon oyster sauce
2   tablespoons hoison sauce
1½ teaspoon Asian chili sauce
1   teaspoon fresh Meyer lemon juice
½   teaspoon sesame oil
1   teaspoon rice vinegar
2   tablespoons water

PULSE everything except water in a food processor. Add 2 tablespoons of water and process again. Consistency should be like mayonnaise.

FILL glass pie plate with hot tap water and work one rice paper at a time. Soak until pliable, about 1 minute. Blot excess water with paper towels. To make the spring roll, layer rice paper, lettuce and basil leaf, rounded teaspoon peanut sauce, chopped peanuts, then cooked shrimp/vegetable mixture. Round rice paper is good for entrée size and triangular is good for appetizer.

Wine Suggestion: Louis Roederer Champagne,
2004 Maculan Pino & Toi or similar

Sun-Dried Tomato Split Pea Dip

This dish is very garlicky, my preference. Begin with less garlic if you just like the overtone of the garlic flavor and add from there to suit your tastes.

1	cup dried, yellow split peas
1	medium yellow onion chopped
1	bay leaf
4	cups water
7	oil packed sun-dried tomato halves, chopped
2	tablespoons red wine vinegar
4	large garlic cloves, peeled and chopped
2	shallots, chopped
4	large basil leaves *(or 1 teaspoon dry basil)*
1½	teaspoons dried oregano
½	teaspoon fresh narrow leaf thyme
½	cup olive oil
	sea salt and pepper to taste

COMBINE peas, onion, and bay leaf with 4 cups water in large saucepan. Bring ingredients to a boil, reduce heat and cover to simmer for 25 more minutes. Drain, discard bay leaf.

PULSE sun-dried tomato, vinegar, garlic, shallots, basil, oregano, and thyme until minced in a food processor. Add cooked peas and onion, pulse until combined. Then with food processor on slow, drizzle olive oil in until smooth paste forms. Serve with pita.

COOKS NOTE: You can substitute red split peas for this dip.

Winter Solstice Paté

This is a quick dish to make with an elegant presentation.
Thanks to Cookie for the first recipe.

2   pounds good liverwurst at room temperature
1   stick of butter, room temperature
8   ounces low fat cream cheese
2   tablespoons Maharajah curry powder*
½   cup fresh flat leaf parsley, chopped
¼   cup minced red onion
½   cup Remy Martin cognac
½   cup golden raisins, chopped

MARINATE raisins in ¼ cup of cognac for 5 minutes. Drain, reserving cognac.

COMBINE all in food processor, except raisins. Pulse ingredients until completed smooth. Fold in raisins and chill. Line bowl with lettuce leaves. Place paté in the middle. Serve with Melba Toasts.

*****COOK'S NOTE:** Curry available from The Spice House, see Resources.

Hearty Hunter Biscuits

*This baking method gives the outside of the biscuit
a little more texture.*

4	cups all-purpose flour
1	rounded tablespoon cream of tartar
2	teaspoons baking soda
1	teaspoon Hunter's Powder *(recipe follows)*
½	teaspoon salt
½	teaspoon sugar
½	cup cold vegetable shortening
1 ¾	cups fresh buttermilk

18

PREHEAT the oven to 475°F.

WHISK flour in a large bowl with the cream of tartar, baking soda, Hunter's Powder, salt and sugar. Using a pastry blender cut in the vegetable shortening until the mixture is combined and crumbly. Add buttermilk and stir with a fork until dough forms a ball.

TURN the dough out onto a lightly floured work surface and knead 3 or 4 times. Roll out the dough to a 1 inch thickness. Using a 2½ inch round biscuit cutter or glass, cut out 12 biscuits. Transfer the biscuits to a non-greased baking sheet, and bake in the bottom third of the oven for 5 minutes. Turn off the heat and let the biscuits sit in the hot oven, without opening the door, for about 10 minutes longer, or until golden and cooked through. Transfer the biscuits to a basket and serve immediately.

Hunter's Powder

2 tablespoons sweet paprika
2 tablespoons kosher salt
2 tablespoons garlic powder
1 tablespoon ground black peppercorns
   (I use Malabar from The Spice House)
1 tablespoon onion powder
1 tablespoon cayenne pepper
1 tablespoon dried oregano
1 tablespoon dried thyme
   (I use narrow-leaf French thyme that I grow)

COMBINE all ingredients and store in glass jar.

COOKS NOTE: These biscuits are great with Thunder Hole Ale Braised Rabbit *(recipe on p. 122)*, or just by themselves.

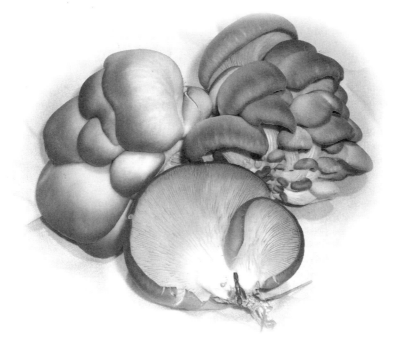

Honey-Graham Dinner Rolls

2   packages dry yeast
½   cup warm water
½   cup honey
½   teaspoon salt
2   eggs
½   cup butter, very soft but not melted
3 ½   cups white flour
½   cup graham flour
2   tablespoons melted butter
    sesame seeds *(optional)*

PREHEAT oven to 375°F.

IN A LARGE BOWL dissolve yeast in warm water. Add the honey, salt, eggs, butter and half the flour. Beat until smooth. Add the remaining flour, mix well. Cover bowl with damp cloth and let rise in warm place until the dough doubles in size, about 1½ hours. Turn on to floured surface, knead for 1 minute. Divide dough into 14 pieces, and form each piece into a ball. Fit the balls into a buttered 10-inch spring form pan and let them rise, covered with a kitchen towel, in a warm place for 45 minutes, or until they are almost double in bulk. Brush the rolls with melted butter and sprinkle with sesame seeds. Bake 15 minutes. Cool on wire rack.

Cinnamon Honey Butter

1   cup butter (room temperature)
½   cup honey
1 ½   teaspoons Vietnamese Cassia "Saigon" Cinnamon
    (available from The Spice House)

COMBINE butter and honey in a small bowl. Beat at high speed until light and fluffy. Add cinnamon and stir to combine.

Whole Wheat and Rosemary Foccacia

My sister-in-law, Jean, says mixing the dough in a bread making machine is cheating. I say if you can make a great bread recipe easier, then do it!

1	cup warm water
1	tablespoon sugar
1	envelope dry yeast
3	tablespoons olive oil
2	cups white flour
½	cups whole wheat
1	teaspoon salt
1	tablespoon rosemary, chopped
1	garlic clove, chopped
1	teaspoon sea salt

PREHEAT oven to 400°F, placing a cooking stone on the bottom rack.

MIX water, sugar and yeast in a bowl, let dissolve for 5 minutes. Stir in 2 tablespoons oil, flour and salt. Add more flour if needed. Knead on dough hook about 8 minutes. Let rise 1 hour in warm place with a covered damp towel.

HEAT remaining tablespoon oil, sauté rosemary and garlic for 2 minutes.

PUNCH dough down and roll out to about 2 inch thickness, brush on rosemary oil and then sprinkle with sea salt. Place on heated stone in oven and bake for 15-20 minutes.

COOK'S NOTE: You can brush a little more olive oil on the crust when it comes out of the oven if you like a softer top.

Jasmine-Ginger Rice

This rice dish is a perfect match with
Rosemary Citrus Chicken (recipe p. 141).

> 3 cups jasmine rice
> 3 tablespoons vegetable oil
> ⅓ cup finely chopped peeled fresh ginger
> 3 large garlic cloves, minced
> 4½ cups chicken broth
> ¾ teaspoon salt
> 1 large bunch fresh cilantro, stems removed and leaves coarsely chopped

22

RINSE rice in large sieve under cold running water until water runs clear. Drain. Heat oil in heavy large saucepan over medium-high heat. Add ginger and garlic; stir until fragrant, about 30 seconds. Add rice and stir 3 minutes. Stir in broth and salt. Sprinkle cilantro over top. Bring to boil. Reduce heat to medium-low; cover and cook until rice is tender, about 18 minutes.

REMOVE from heat; let stand covered 10 minutes. Fluff rice with fork. Transfer to bowl and serve.

Maine Maple Beans

Saturday night beans never tasted so good.

2   pounds of dry small pea beans
    (*Jacob Cattle or your favorite*)
1   medium onion
½   cup packed brown sugar
½   pound salt pork
½   teaspoon dry mustard
½   teaspoon ginger
2   cups dark maple syrup
    salt and pepper to taste

WASH the dry beans, place them in a pot, and cover with water, about 6 inches above the beans. Soak overnight.

IN THE MORNING, bring to a boil. Lower the heat and simmer about 10 minutes or until the skins slough off the beans when you blow on them. Drain the water off and reserve. Place the onion in the bottom of a bean pot and pour the beans into the pot. Slice the salt pork in quarters and place it rind side up on top of the beans. In a bowl, mix the maple syrup, dry mustard, ginger, salt, and pepper. Add one cup of the water the beans were cooked in, stir together and pour the mixture over the beans. Add more of the bean water to the pot until it reaches one inch above the beans.

BAKE in the oven for eight hours at 275°F.

Bread and Butter Pickles

I made three different batches before I came up with the one I really liked. I hope you like it too!

16   cups pickling cucumbers,
      sliced ⅛ thick with skin on
2   large white onions sliced thin
2   whole garlic cloves
5   cups cold water
½   cup pickling salt
4   cups sugar
3   cups white vinegar
2   tablespoons yellow mustard seed
1   teaspoon celery seed
1   teaspoon turmeric

SOAK cucumbers, onions and garlic in salt and water. Let stand overnight. Rinse thoroughly in cold water. Remove garlic.

MIX remaining ingredients in large stockpot and bring to a boil. Add cucumbers and onions and boil until tender, about 12 minutes.

LADLE into hot, sterilized jars. Tighten and turn upside down on towel. Cool overnight and store in a dry cupboard, pantry or larder.

Maple-Ginger Roasted Pecans

I use my Uncle Gary's homemade maple syrup.
It tastes awesome!

3 cups of whole pecans
3 inch piece of fresh ginger,
    peeled and sliced very thin
½ cup dark maple syrup
3 tablespoons warm water

PREHEAT oven to 325°F.

COMBINE ginger, syrup and water in a wide, heavy saucepan. Heat through, turn off heat and let ginger steep for 30 minutes. Add pecans and simmer over low heat until nuts have absorbed the liquids, stirring continually. Make sure pecans are not more than doubled on top of each other. Spread on greased cookie sheet and bake for about 10 minutes. Stir several times while baking so they do not stick to each other. Cool and store in air tight container.

Fresh Basil Pesto

1 cup fresh basil leaves
¼ cup parsley
¼ cup grated Parmesan cheese
¼ cup toasted pine nuts
3 large garlic cloves, minced
¼ cup Portuguese olive oil

PROCESS in food processor until it pastes. Freeze extra.

Kate's Spicy Mango Paste

2 cans of mangos, drained and chopped
with juice reserved
1 tablespoon dry mustard
½ cup canola oil
1 tablespoon Chris's Hot Sauce *(recipe p. 183)*
1 tablespoon raisins, chopped very fine
1 teaspoon sea salt
1 tablespoon garlic pureed
1 teaspoon ground Tellicherry peppercorns

DRAIN canned mango and reserve the juices.

PUREE all ingredients. Simmer in a sauce pan for one hour. If you need more moisture while cooking add reserved mango juice, a little at a time. It should be pasty when done.

COOK'S NOTE: Mix with mayonnaise for delicious chicken or turkey salad sandwiches. I use it to spice up pasta salads, or mix with cream cheese to spread on crackers with roasted peppers.

Zucchini Relish

Thanks, George, for this wonderful recipe that I use for my Zucchini Tartar Sauce, with some slight changes of course!

10	cups shredded zucchini
4	cups onion, chopped fine
2	sweet red peppers, chopped
2 ½	cups white vinegar
6	cups sugar
1	teaspoon turmeric powder
1	teaspoon dry mustard
2	teaspoons celery seed
½	teaspoon ground black pepper
2	teaspoons mustard seed
3	teaspoons corn starch to thicken

COMBINE zucchini and onions in large bowl. Mix in salt and let stand overnight. The next morning drain and thoroughly rinse. Place in large stockpot. Add the remaining ingredients and bring to a boil for 10 minutes.

POUR relish into sterilized jars, seal and process in hot water bath for 20 minutes.

Yields 8 pints.

Salads

Indonesian Rice Salad

Vegetable Pasta Salad

Red Potato Dill Salad

Homemade Herbed Croutons

Asian Salad Dressing

Steamed Asparagus Dressing

Balsamic Vinaigrette

Creamy Blue Cheese Dressing

Creamy Dill Dressing

Herbes de Provence Salad Dressing

Kate's Caesar Dressing

Pan Asian Dressing

Meyer Lemon Truffle Vinaigrette

Versatile Vinaigrette

Warm Black Fly Vinaigrette

Warm White Balsamic Dressing

Indonesian Rice Salad

*This is the number one most requested salad I've ever made.
It is great warm or chilled.*

2	cups brown rice
⅓	cup peanut oil
3	tablespoons sesame seed oil
½	cup orange juice
2	tablespoons tamari (soy sauce)
1	teaspoon salt
1	cup crushed pineapple
1	tablespoon honey
3	scallions, minced
½	pound mung bean sprouts
½	cup raisins
½	cup chopped peanuts
½	cup toasted cashews
2	tablespoons sesame seeds
1½	cups red, orange, and yellow peppers, diced
1	cup sliced water chestnuts

COOK brown rice in 3 cups water.

MIX peanut oil, sesame seed oil, orange juice, tamari, salt, crushed pineapple and honey to make the dressing.

ADD scallions, bean sprouts, raisins, chopped peanuts, toasted cashews, sesame seeds, peppers, and water chestnuts to hot, cooked rice. Pour all the dressing over the rice and vegetables, mix and enjoy.

COOK'S NOTE: This is a perfect salad to gorge on at a picnic.

Vegetable Pasta Salad

A great salad for summer events.

12 ounces tri-color pasta
¼ cup red onion, chopped
1 cup broccoli, chopped
¼ cup each red, yellow and orange pepper, chopped
3 eggs
⅓ cup white sugar
1 tablespoon Dijon style mustard
4 tablespoons cider vinegar
3 tablespoons prepared mayonnaise
1 tablespoon fresh, chopped dill
   Salt and freshly, ground pepper to taste

COOK pasta, drain and put in bowl. Add red onion, broccoli and peppers.

WHISK eggs, sugar, mustard, and vinegar on medium high in a small saucepan. Stir constantly to prevent scorching on bottom. Remove pan from heat as soon as egg mixture becomes thick and whisk in mayonnaise.

SPRINKLE pasta mixture with fresh chopped dill and stir in dressing. Delicious served warm or chilled.

COOK'S NOTE: This dressing is great on red potato salad too!

Red Potato Dill Salad

Delicious served warm or cold.

8 medium red potatoes, cooked and cut into chunks
1 medium yellow onion chopped
2 tablespoons zucchini or sweet pickle relish

COMBINE and set aside.

Dressing

3 eggs
½ cup sugar
2 tablespoons Dijon style mustard
4 tablespoons apple cider vinegar
3 tablespoons prepared mayonnaise
1 tablespoon fresh dill

WHISK ingredients, except mayonnaise and dill, in a sauce pan over medium-high heat. Remove from stove as soon as it begins to thicken, stir in mayonnaise and dill. Pour over potato salad and sprinkle with fresh dill.

Homemade Herbed Croutons

1 baguette or small loaf bread
2 tablespoons melted butter
1 tablespoon extra virgin olive oil
½ teaspoon dried parsley*
1 teaspoon minced garlic
½ teaspoon sea salt

PREHEAT the oven to 375°F .

CUT the bread into squares. Combine melted butter and olive oil. Toss bread squares in the oil, melted butter and seasonings. Place on a baking sheet in 1 layer. Bake, tossing several times until they are golden brown, crispy on the outside and a little soft inside, 10 to 15 minutes. Cool at room temperature and reserve. Store in airtight container.

*COOK'S NOTE: Substitutions for parsley – thyme, rosemary, chervil or your favorite herbs.

Asian Salad Dressing

Thanks to Allison's suggestions on this dressing I was able to create a new marinade.

⅔	cup peanut oil
1	tablespoon toasted sesame seeds
4	garlic cloves, minced
¼	cup rice wine vinegar
2	tablespoons soy sauce
2	tablespoons dark sesame oil
1	teaspoon orange zest

COMBINE ingredients in glass jar and shake. Serve over spring greens, shredded carrots, red onion ringlets, and pumpkin seeds. Refrigerate unused portion.

COOK'S NOTE: Great for marinating fish, chicken or tofu.

Steamed Asparagus Dressing

This dressing makes the asparagus taste "extra fresh!"

 6 tablespoons Meyer lemon olive oil
 2 tablespoons white wine vinegar
 1 tablespoon white wine
 2 tablespoons chopped fresh parsley
 2 tablespoons chopped fresh basil
 1 garlic clove, minced
 ¼ teaspoon dried crushed red pepper
 ¼ teaspoon dried oregano
 ¼ teaspoon sea salt

WHISK ingredients together and drizzle over hot, steamed asparagus.

Balsamic Vinaigrette

This is a great basic recipe if you enjoy the flavor of balsamic vinegar.

 ½ cup extra-virgin olive oil
 3 tablespoons balsamic vinegar
 ½ teaspoon dried thyme leaves
 ½ teaspoon dried oregano leaves
 1½ teaspoon freshly ground black pepper

PLACE vinegar in a bowl and whisk in extra-virgin olive oil in a slow stream to combine. Add seasonings and pepper and whisk again to distribute the herbs and spice throughout the dressing.

Creamy Blue Cheese Dressing

My whole family loves blue cheese - this one is a winner!

1	large garlic clove, minced
1	tablespoon Dijon style mustard
1	tablespoon fresh squeezed lemon juice
½	teaspoon kosher salt
¼	teaspoon white pepper
2	tablespoons white wine vinegar
⅓	cup Portuguese olive oil *(or extra virgin olive oil)*
⅓	cup sour cream
1 ¼	cups crumbled Stilton blue cheese
	(or your favorite dry blue cheese)

IN A FOOD PROCESSOR blend the garlic, mustard, lemon juice, vinegar, salt and pepper to taste. With the motor running add the oil and blend the mixture until it is combined well. Add the sour cream, and ½ cup blue cheese, blend the dressing until it is combined well, and transfer it to a bowl. Stir in the additional cheese. The dressing needs to sit and absorb flavors.

COOK'S NOTE: To thin this dressing add whole milk, one tablespoon at a time.

Creamy Dill Dressing

3 eggs
1 tablespoon dill seed
1 tablespoon dill weed
3 tablespoons white vinegar
1 teaspoon salt
½ teaspoon freshly ground black pepper
2 cups canola or vegetable oil
1 tablespoon honey

COMBINE all ingredients, except oil and honey, in a blender or small food processor. Turn blender on low and drizzle in oil and honey. This gives the dressing a thicker body. Refrigerate up to a week. Makes 3 cups dressing.

Herbes de Provence Salad Dressing

¼ cup olive oil
3 tablespoon red wine vinegar
2 tablespoons freshly chopped flat leaf parsley
1 tablespoon minced garlic
2 teaspoons Herbes de Provence*
¼ teaspoon kosher or sea salt
⅛ teaspoon freshly ground black pepper

COMBINE all ingredients in glass jar and shake well.

*COOK'S NOTE: Herbes de Provence is typically made up of dried thyme, rosemary, summer savory and bay leaves. *(recipe p. 185, or store bought)*

Kate's Caesar Dressing

*When my nieces come for a visit (Kirstie, Ashley, Katie and Tracy),
I usually have to send them packing with a bottle of my
homemade Caesar Dressing (or Rice Krispie Squares!)*

1 teaspoon Meyer lemon zest
3 garlic cloves, minced
1 teaspoon Tellicherry peppercorns, ground
½ teaspoon sea salt
1 teaspoon anchovy paste
1 tablespoon fish sauce
1 cup extra-virgin olive oil
½ cup lemon juice
3 tablespoons white wine *(Chardonnay)*
1 medium egg white

COMBINE all ingredients in glass jar and shake vigorously. Store
unused portion of the dressing in the refrigerator.

Pan-Asian Dressing

⅔ cup peanut oil
⅓ cup sesame oil
3 large garlic cloves, minced
⅓ cup red wine vinegar
3 tablespoons soy
¼ cup minced, roasted peanuts

COMBINE all ingredients in glass jar, shake and serve.

Meyer Lemon Truffle Vinaigrette

A partner in our a cappella business has a Meyer lemon tree in his back yard in San Francisco. After making recipes with this sweet lemon, I just can't go back. Thanks Deke!

3   tablespoon Meyer lemon juice
    (or regular lemon juice)
2   cloves garlic, minced
2   tablespoons red wine vinegar
1   anchovy fillet
1   tablespoon Dijon style mustard
1   teaspoon Worcestershire sauce
2   dashes hot sauce
    salt and pepper
1   egg yolk
1   tablespoon truffle olive oil
½   cup extra virgin olive oil
    grated Parmesan

IN A SMALL FOOD PROCESSOR, add garlic, lemon juice, vinegar, anchovy fillet, mustard, Worcestershire sauce, hot sauce, salt, pepper, and egg yolk and process for 15 seconds. With the processor running, slowly drizzle in the truffle oil and the olive oil *(this process thickens the dressing and makes it look creamy)*.

Versatile Vinaigrette

3   tablespoons brown sugar
3   tablespoons balsamic vinegar
¼   cup red wine
2   tablespoons Dijon style mustard
2   tablespoons fresh rosemary, chopped
1   teaspoon coarse salt
1   teaspoon herbed pepper*
3   tablespoons Worcestershire sauce
2   tablespoons soy sauce
1   cup extra virgin olive oil

COMBINE all ingredients, except oil in a bowl and stir.
Whisk oil into bowl. Pour over salad.

COOK'S NOTE: Great over fresh greens, goat cheese and sliced
thin red onion. Complements red meat dishes: lamb, goat,
moose, deer . . . you get the picture.

Tortolla herbed pepper, see Resources.

Warm Black Fly Vinaigrette

Unofficial state bird dressing.

1 cup canola oil
⅓ cup honey
2 tablespoons red wine vinegar
2 teaspoons lemon juice
1 teaspoon Dijon style mustard
1 tablespoon dried black flies *(substitute: poppy seeds)*
1 teaspoon minced garlic
⅛ teaspoon cayenne pepper
¼ teaspoon sea salt
¼ teaspoon black pepper

WHISK all ingredients in a saucepan over low heat until combined. Pour immediately onto salad.

COOK'S NOTE: Great on mixed greens, red onion, goat cheese and roasted pecans.

Warm White Balsamic Dressing

A surprise taste because of the lack of color in the balsamic vinegar; this is an eye opener for your guests. It fools the taste buds.

½ cup extra-virgin olive oil
2 garlic cloves, chopped
½ cup white balsamic vinegar
½ teaspoon honey
¼ teaspoon salt
¼ teaspoon black pepper

HEAT OIL and garlic in a small pan over moderate heat. Simmer garlic in oil to infuse the flavor. Remove the garlic from the oil and transfer oil to a small bowl. Wipe the pan and return to heat. Add balsamic vinegar and honey. Raise heat to high and reduce vinegar by half, about 30 seconds. Stream oil into saucepan and whisk to combine with vinegar. Season salad with salt and pepper then drizzle dressing over the salad.

Vegetables

Steamed Fiddleheads

Maple Glazed Carrots

Anise Carrots

Garam Masala Eggplant

Braised Shallots and Carrots

Asparagus and Oyster Mushrooms

Asparagus and Sun-Dried Tomato Tart

Beer Battered Onion Rings

Sweet Pepper Saffron Grill

Blue Hubbard Squash Soup with Croutons

Carrot Dill Soup

Moose River Corn Chowder

Roasted Two Tomato Basil Soup

Spiced Carrot Soup

Wild Mushroom Soup

Sweet and Spicy Pumpkin Soup

Jasmine Rice with Ginger and Cilantro

Saffron Rice

Mexican Lasagna

White Sweet Potatoes Au Gratin

Artwork by Gail Cleveland

Steamed Fiddleheads

Steaming the fiddleheads offers a wonderful contrast
of flavor with the vinegar, salt and butter.

3   cups cleaned fiddleheads
¼   cup apple cider vinegar
½   cup water
1   teaspoon salt
2   tablespoons butter

PLACE clean fiddle heads in steamer over vinegar and water. Steam fiddleheads for 10 minutes. Season with butter and salt to taste.

Maple Glazed Carrots

1   pound of carrots, peeled and sliced
3   tablespoons butter
¼   cup Maine maple syrup
½   teaspoon powdered ginger
5   thin slices of fresh ginger

STEAM carrots in water and sliced fresh ginger slices. Empty water, add butter, maple syrup, ginger and heat through. Add cooked carrots and simmer until carrots are glazed and warmed.

Anise Carrots

You'll be pleasantly surprised at this simple spice suggestion for carrots.

- 1   pound of carrots, cut julienne
- 1   star of anise
- 1   cup water

PLACE carrots in a steamer, with water and anise star in bottom pot. Steam the carrots for 20 minutes. Salt, butter and enjoy!

COOK'S NOTE: A julienne carrot is cut in 3 inch lengths and then in matchstick cuts.

Garam Masala Eggplant

Great as a side dish or appetizer.

- 1 ½   pounds small eggplants cut in 5 inch long pieces and quartered
- ½   teaspoon turmeric
- ⅛   teaspoon sea salt
- 1   cup olive oil
- 1 ½   teaspoons fresh garlic, minced
- 1 ½   inch piece of fresh, gingerroot, grated
- 1   tablespoon Garam Masala *(recipe p. 184, or store bought)*
- ¼   teaspoon cayenne pepper

HEAT oil in skillet and fry eggplants on medium for 7 minutes, turning frequently. Add remaining ingredients and cook uncovered for 10 more minutes.

Braised Shallots and Carrots

1 ½	cups shallots, thinly sliced
6	medium carrots, peeled
2	tablespoons olive oil
2	tablespoons unsalted butter
1	teaspoon kosher salt
2	14.5-ounce cans whole tomatoes, cut into ½-inch pieces
½	cup of the tomato juice from the cans
5	large cloves garlic, sliced
1	teaspoon fresh, minced ginger
½	teaspoon thyme
½	teaspoon parsley
⅛	teaspoon cayenne
¼	cup water
3	tablespoons chopped fresh flat-leaf parsley

PREHEAT the oven to 350°F.

CUT carrots in half lengthwise and into 2-inch long pieces. Heat the butter and olive oil in a sauce pan over medium heat. Add the shallots and cook, stirring occasionally, until softened and slightly browned, about 5 minutes. Remove the shallots and set them aside. Add carrots and salt, cook about 12 minutes, stirring occasionally, until the carrots are lightly browned. Add the tomatoes and their juices, along with the garlic, ginger, thyme, parsley and cayenne. Stir in the shallots and ¼ cup water. Cover the pot, put it in the oven, and let cook until very tender, 20 to 25 minutes. Sprinkle with parsley and serve. *Serves 4*

COOK'S NOTE: You can substitute olive oil with blood orange olive oil and minced ginger with 3 large orange zest strips. Remove strips before adding shallots.

Asparagus and Oyster Mushrooms

*Fresh tarragon, if you can get it, adds a level
of flavor that keeps on giving.*

2	pounds asparagus, cut diagonally in 4-inch lengths
2	tablespoons unsalted butter
1 ½	pounds oyster mushrooms, quartered
¼	teaspoon salt
¼	teaspoon pepper
2	shallots, minced
¼	cup dry white wine *(Pinot Blanc or dry Riesling)*
½	cup chicken stock or canned low-sodium broth
¾	cup light cream
1	tablespoon tarragon, minced

IN A MEDIUM SAUCEPAN of boiling salted water, blanch the asparagus until bright green, about 2 minutes. Drain, refresh in a bowl of ice water; drain again.

MELT the butter in a large skillet. Add the mushrooms, salt and pepper and cook over medium heat until browned on the bottom, about 3 minutes. Stir the mushrooms and cook until tender, about 4 minutes longer. Add the shallots and cook, stirring, about 3 minutes. Add the wine and cook until evaporated, about 30 seconds. Add the chicken stock and asparagus and simmer until the liquid has reduced to 2 tablespoons, about 2 minutes. Stir in cream and tarragon and simmer over low heat until slightly thickened, about 5 minutes.

Asparagus and Sun-Dried Tomato Tart

1 tablespoon unsalted butter
1 tablespoon olive oil
1 shallot, finely chopped
1 bunch asparagus, ends trimmed off,
    cut at a diagonal into 2-inch pieces
½ pound puff pastry, defrosted
½ pound soft goat cheese
9 sun-dried tomatoes, cut in thin strips lengthwise
1 teaspoon fresh thyme
    salt and freshly ground black pepper
1 egg white mixed with ½ teaspoon cold water

PRE-HEAT the oven to 450°F.

IN A MEDIUM SAUCEPAN, melt butter and add oil. Add the shallot to the pan and sauté for 1 minute. Add the asparagus and cook over medium-high heat until the asparagus is crisp-tender, about 5 min. Remove the pan from the heat. Add sun-dried tomatoes and mix in with the asparagus and shallot.

ON A LIGHTLY FLOURED piece of kitchen parchment roll out the pastry to a 10x16-inch rectangle. Transfer the pastry and parchment paper onto a baking sheet.

USING YOUR FINGERS, pat the goat cheese onto the pastry, spreading it as evenly as you can and leaving a 1-inch border around the edge. Sprinkle the thyme, then the asparagus, shallot and sun-dried tomato mixture evenly over the goat cheese. Season with salt and pepper.

BRUSH the edge of the tart with the egg wash. Bake until the pastry is golden brown, 20 to 25 min. Let cool slightly and serve warm.

COOK'S NOTES: This is a great recipe for testing your favorite combination of flavors. How about Saga blue cheese, pear and red onions?

Beer Battered Onion Rings

The first time I tried this recipe I was running a restaurant down in the Old Port. I make it with an ale now, what do you think?

1	cup flour
¼	teaspoon salt
¼	teaspoon celery salt
⅛	teaspoon black pepper
½	teaspoon sugar
1	cup Todd's Special Summer Ale, flat*
1	large sweet onion, sliced in ½ inch rings and separated

PREHEAT vegetable oil in large fryer.

COMBINE all dry ingredients, except onion, in a bowl. Whisk in ale just before you are ready to deep fry onion rings. Dip onion rings in batter, shake excess batter off and deep fry until golden.

*Ale from Bar Harbor Brewing Company, see Resources.

Sweet Pepper Saffron Grill

Sometimes I throw fresh shrimp in the marinade, which are great on the grill.

2 tablespoons canola oil
4 large shallots, minced
¼ cup soy sauce
3 tablespoons sweet curry powder
½ cup dry white wine
½ teaspoon saffron threads
1 large red pepper
1 yellow pepper

SAUTÉ shallots in canola oil until browned in saucepan, about 3 minutes. Add remaining ingredients, except peppers. Mix and warm together.

CUT the peppers into 2 inch pieces. Add to shallot mixture and marinate overnight in the refrigerator. Toss the vegetables periodically to keep coated.

THREAD the marinated vegetables onto your pre-soaked skewers.

GRILL until vegetables are cooked through.

COOK'S NOTE: Soak wooden skewers for 2 hours before skewing vegetables on them. This will prevent skewers from catching on fire and vegetables from falling off.

Blue Hubbard Squash Soup with Croutons

How many different recipes can I make when the harvest is in?
Many with a huge squash.

4 tablespoons unsalted butter
2 tablespoons roasted pumpkin seed oil *(or peanut oil)*
3 pounds blue hubbard squash, skinned, seeded and chopped
1 sweet onion, chopped
3 cups chicken stock
1 tablespoon dark brown sugar
½ cup light cream
¼ teaspoon Hungarian paprika
⅛ teaspoon nutmeg, grated
½ teaspoon sea salt

MELT butter, add oil and onion. Sauté for 3 minutes. Add pumpkin, coat and sauté for another 5 minutes. Add stock, brown sugar and bring to boil and then simmer 30 minutes. Use food processor or emulsifier to blend and return to pan.

STIR IN CREAM, paprika and nutmeg. Season with more salt if needed.

Croutons

4 slices bread
¼ cup vegetable oil
½ teaspoon paprika

CUT shapes in sliced bread. Fry in oil until golden brown on both sides. Drain on paper towel and dust with paprika.

COOK'S NOTE: This recipe can be made and frozen for a winter dinner. Add the cream after you unfreeze it.

Carrot Dill Soup

Here's a quick, porridge style soup that will stick to your bones in the winter months. Try it with my Honey-Graham Rolls (recipe p. 20).

1   tablespoon butter
2   tablespoons canola oil
1   onion, peeled and diced
3   cloves garlic, minced
1   teaspoon salt
1   teaspoon brown sugar
1   tablespoon fresh dill, chopped
1   pound carrots, peeled and chopped
1   quart chicken or vegetable stock

52

MELT butter in heavy Dutch oven. Add oil, onion and garlic. Sauté 3 minutes. Add carrots and sauté for another 5 minutes. Add spices, stock, rice and bring to boil and then simmer 30 minutes. Use food processor or emulsifier to blend and return to pan. Season with more salt, if needed.

Wine: Chardonnay or Chenin Blanc

Moose River Corn Chowder

Five girlfriends from USM were hiking Bald Mountain with six guys from Jackman, resulting in a very hungry crew. Add my brother's somewhat empty cupboard and you have meal improvisation. The sweet condensed milk added a light, sweet richness to this chowder.

½ pound bacon, chopped
1 large onion, chopped
1 cup water
3 cups potatoes, diced
2 teaspoons salt
1 teaspoon black pepper
2 cans cream style corn
2 cups frozen corn
3 tablespoons sweet condensed milk
2 cups whole milk
2 tablespoons butter

SAUTÉ bacon in a large kettle until cooked. Remove bacon and reserve for garnish. Add onions, cook slowly until translucent. Add water, potatoes, salt and pepper. Lower heat and cook potatoes until tender, about 15 minutes. Add corn, milks and butter. Simmer very low for one hour to develop flavor. Garnish with bacon bits.

Roasted Two Tomato Basil Soup

3 pounds ripe Roma plum tomatoes cut in half
2 pounds ripe Yellow Taxi tomatoes cut in half
¼ cup garlic olive oil
1 tablespoon kosher salt
1 teaspoon freshly ground black pepper
2 tablespoons olive oil
1 cup yellow onion, chopped
1 cup sweet onion, chopped
5 garlic cloves, minced
2 tablespoons unsalted butter
4 cups fresh basil leaves, packed
1 teaspoon fresh thyme leaves
1 quart chicken stock or water
basil leaves for garnish, filigreed*

PREHEAT the oven to 400°F.

TOSS together the tomatoes, ¼ cup olive oil, salt, and pepper. Spread the tomatoes in 1 layer on a baking sheet with sides and roast for 45 minutes.

IN LARGE STOCKPOT, sauté the onions and garlic with 2 tablespoons of olive oil and the butter for 10 minutes, until the onions start to brown. Add the basil, thyme, and chicken stock. Add the oven-roasted tomatoes, including the liquid on the baking sheet. Bring to a boil and simmer uncovered for 40 minutes. Pass through a mill to remove seeds and skins. Ladle into soup bowls and top with filigreed basil leaves.

*COOK'S NOTE: Filigreed basil leaves: roll leaf to form a tube, cut on the diagonal in thin strips.

Spiced Carrot Soup

The roasted pumpkin seed oil gives this soup
another dimension of depth.

1	tablespoon butter
2	tablespoons roasted pumpkin oil *(or peanut oil)*
1	onion, peeled and diced
3	cloves garlic, minced
1	teaspoon salt
½	teaspoon black pepper
1	teaspoon brown sugar
1 ½	teaspoons roasted, ground cumin
¾	teaspoon ground coriander seeds
1	pound carrots, peeled and chopped
¼	cup raw white rice
1	bay leaf
1	quart chicken stock, vegetable stock, or water

MELT butter in heavy Dutch oven. Add oil, onion and garlic. Sauté
3 minutes. Add carrots and brown sugar, coat and sauté for another
5 minutes. Add spices, stock, rice and bring to boil, cover and
simmer 30 minutes. Remove bay leaf. Use food processor or
emulsifier to blend and return to pan. Season with more salt,
if needed.

COOK'S NOTE: This soup has a porridge style thickness. To thin,
add more stock or for creamier texture add ½ cup of whole milk.

Wine: 1999 Robert Mondavi PNX Pinot Noir

Wild Mushroom Soup

Mushrooms have such amazing flavors when freshly picked!

8 tablespoons unsalted butter
1 cup shallots, minced
4 garlic cloves, minced
½ teaspoon fresh nutmeg, grated
1 pound white button mushrooms, sliced ¼ inch thick
1 pound Crimini mushrooms, sliced ¼ inch thick
1 pound pearl oyster mushrooms, sliced ¼ inch thick
4 cups chicken stock *(homemade works best for this recipe)*
2 cups hot water
1 ounce dried porcini mushrooms, rinsed well
¾ cup dry sherry
½ cup heavy cream
   juice of 1 lemon
   salt and pepper to taste

MELT butter in large stockpot over medium heat. When foaming subsides, add shallots and sauté for 4 minutes. Stir in garlic and nutmeg and cook for 1 minute. Increase heat to medium-high, add sliced mushrooms (not porcinis) and stir to coat with butter. Cook until mushrooms release some liquid, about 9-10 minutes, stirring occasionally. Reduce heat to low, cover pot, stir occasionally until mushrooms have released all their liquid, about 20 minutes. Add stock, water, and porcini mushrooms and simmer about 20 more minutes.

PUREE soup in food processor or use emulsifier, while still hot, until smooth. Stir in sherry and cream. Simmer over low heat for 10 minutes. Add lemon juice and season with salt and pepper. Serve immediately. *Serves 8*

Wine: Sebastopol Pinot Noir (a meaty Pinot Noir)

Sweet and Spicy Pumpkin Soup

I cannot express the difference made using the roasted pumpkin seed oil. You'll have to taste for yourself.

3	pounds pumpkin, seeded, peeled and chopped
¼	cup roasted pumpkin seed oil *(or peanut oil)*
1	tablespoon garlic, minced
1	tablespoon ginger, minced
1	tablespoon shallots, minced
⅛	teaspoon red pepper flakes
½	teaspoon Chris's hot sauce *(recipe p. 183)*
1	teaspoon salt
½	teaspoon freshly ground white pepper
½	teaspoon turmeric
2	tablespoons honey
7	cups chicken stock
½	cup heavy cream

HEAT oil in Dutch oven, add garlic and sauté for 3 minutes. Add pumpkin and coat, sauté for another 5 minutes. Add remaining ingredients except cream. Bring to a boil and then simmer 30 minutes. Use food processor or emulsifier to blend and return to pan. Add cream and season with more salt, if needed.

Wine: Ridge Zinfandel

Jasmine Rice with Ginger and Cilantro

This dish goes great with Spicy Island Venison (recipe p. 115).

This dish goes great with Spicy Island Venison (recipe p. 115).

    3   cups jasmine rice
    3   tablespoons vegetable oil
    ⅓   cup finely chopped peeled fresh ginger
    3   large garlic cloves, minced
 4 ½   cups chicken broth*
    ¾   teaspoon salt
    1   large bunch fresh cilantro, 2 inches of bottom
        stems trimmed and discarded, tops and remaining
        stems coarsely chopped

RINSE rice in large sieve under cold running water until water runs clear. Drain. Heat oil in heavy large saucepan over medium-high heat. Add ginger and garlic; stir until fragrant, about 30 seconds. Add rice and stir 3 minutes. Stir in broth and salt. Sprinkle in cilantro.. Bring to boil. Reduce heat to medium-low; cover and cook until rice is tender, about 18 minutes. Remove from heat; let stand covered 10 minutes. Fluff rice with fork. Transfer to bowl and serve.

*COOK'S NOTE: I use broth in a recipe when I don't need as much salt and I use stock when I do want more salt.

Saffron Rice

1 tablespoon butter
1 tablespoon minced red onion
1 cup jasmine rice
2 cups chicken stock
½ teaspoon salt
2 tablespoons raisins
⅛ teaspoon crumbled saffron

SAUTÉ onions in butter for 3 minutes. Add the remaining ingredients and bring to a boil.

COVER, reduce heat and simmer for 18 minutes.

59

COOK'S NOTE: I let the saffron sit in the stock for 30 minutes before I cook this dish. I feel the flavor exhibits more depth.

Mexican Lasagna

2 tablespoons garlic olive oil
1 large onion, chopped
1 red pepper, chopped
1 green pepper, chopped
1 jalapeño pepper, chopped
1 dried habenero
3 tablespoons chopped garlic
2 medium zucchini, chopped
1 teaspoon salt
1 teaspoon black pepper
2 teaspoons roasted, ground cumin
2 tablespoons chili powder
½ teaspoon cayenne pepper
1 tablespoon Mexican oregano
¼ teaspoon cinnamon
1 tablespoon pureed chipotle peppers
1 tablespoon Ancho chile pepper, chopped
2 28-ounce cans diced tomatoes
2 cups whole frozen corn, thawed
2 cans black beans, drained and rinsed
6 cups shredded cheddar cheese
   homemade lasagna noodles

PREHEAT oven to 350° F.

SAUTÉ first 7 ingredients until slightly tender, add zucchini and all spices, cook on medium for 10 minutes. Add diced tomatoes, corn and black beans. Cook for 45 minutes on medium for spices to meld.

TO MAKE NOODLES: I use homemade noodles and add 2 teaspoons homemade salsa seasoning and 2 teaspoons Mexican oregano to the dough mixture. You can substitute salsa and tortilla wraps torn in pieces to fit the pan.

LAYER in 9" x 12" pan; ½ cup sauce, noodles, sauce, noodles, cheese, noodles, sauce, noodles, sauce and cheese. Bake for 1 hour covered. Remove aluminum foil and bake 20 minutes to brown top.

White Sweet Potatoes au Gratin

     2   tablespoons unsalted butter
     4   garlic cloves, finely chopped
     1   shallot, finely chopped
         sea salt and freshly ground black pepper
     2   pounds white sweet potatoes, peeled and thinly sliced
         (about ⅛ inch)
 2 ½   cups heavy cream
     2   cups grated Parmesan
     ¼   cup chopped fresh chives, finely chopped for garnish

PREHEAT the oven to 375°F.

GENEROUSLY butter the bottom and sides of a 9"x 13" casserole dish. In a large bowl, combine the potatoes, salt and pepper and ½ the garlic and toss to coat. Pour potatoes into buttered baking pan.

MELT 2 tablespoons of butter in frying pan. When it has melted add remaining ½ of the garlic and the shallot, cook until softened. Add cream and stir over medium heat for 5 minutes then add 1 cup Parmesan and heat through until melted and warm. Pour over potatoes and sprinkle the remaining Parmesan cheese.

COVER dish with aluminum foil. Bake for 1 hour. Remove foil and bake for 30 minutes or until golden brown. Let rest for 10 minutes before serving. Garnish with fresh chives.

COOK'S NOTE: You can layer the coated potatoes into the baking dish for a more elegant presentation.

Seafood

Downeast Lobster Mac 'N Cheese
Real Maine Lobster Rolls
Grown-Up Mac and Cheese with Maine Lobster
Lobster Newberg
Asian Lobster Stuffed Sole
Baked Maine Lobster Dip
Maine Lobster Salad With Spicy Lemon Dressing
Lobster with Nutmeg Vinaigrette
Lobster Stock
Simple Maine Lobster Stew
Sherry-Ginger Lobster Sauce
Cedar Smoked Salmon
Char Provençal
Crab Cakes with Zucchini Tartar Sauce
Downeast Seafood Gumbo
Maine Seafood Gumbo
Grilled Halibut Glaze
Hot and Sweet Grilled Salmon
Layered Maine Shrimp Dish
Rocky Coast Clam Chowder
Grilled Swordfish with Mango Salsa
Salmon Peppered Jerky
Seafood Fettuccini
Shrimp Jambalaya
Steamed Mussels with Harbor Lighthouse Ale

63

Downeast Lobster Mac 'N Cheese

This recipe had all my testers in lobster heaven. It's worth the time!

1   2-pound live Maine lobster
2   tablespoons olive oil, divided
12   large shrimp, peeled, deveined, shells reserved
1   cup chopped onion
¾   cup chopped peeled carrots
2   garlic cloves, peeled, flattened
1   bay leaf
1   tablespoon tomato paste
¼   cup cognac *(or brandy)*
3   cups water
4   tablespoons butter, divided
2   tablespoons all purpose flour
½   cup whipping cream
1 ½   cups grated Fontina cheese *(about 6 ounces)*
8   ounces small shell pasta
6   ounces fresh crabmeat, claws not body meat
2   tablespoons chopped fresh chives

LOBSTER STOCK: Plunge lobster headfirst into pot of boiling water; boil 4 minutes. Using tongs, transfer to cutting board. Cut off tail and claws. Crack tail and claws and remove meat. Cut meat into ½-inch pieces. Cut body and shells into 2-inch pieces. Chill meat; reserve shells.

HEAT 1 tablespoon oil in heavy large skillet over medium-high heat. Add lobster body, lobster shells, and shrimp shells to skillet and sauté 4 minutes. Add onion and next 3 ingredients; sauté 6 minutes. Add tomato paste; stir 1 minute. Remove from heat; stir in cognac. Add 3 cups water; bring to boil. Reduce heat, cover, and simmer 30 minutes.

STRAIN mixture into bowl, pressing on solids to extract liquid; discard solids. Set stock aside. Heat 1 tablespoon oil in same skillet over medium-high heat. Add shrimp; sauté until just opaque in center, about 3 minutes. Cool slightly. Coarsely chop shrimp. Melt 2 tablespoons butter in large saucepan over medium heat. Add flour, stir 1 minute. Add stock and cream, simmer until sauce is reduced to 2 cups, about 5 minutes. Add cheese, stir until smooth. Season with salt and pepper. Remove from heat.

MEANWHILE, cook pasta in large pot of boiling salted water until just tender but still firm to bite. Drain. Stir lobster, shrimp, pasta, crabmeat, and 2 tablespoons butter into sauce. Stir over medium-low heat until heated through, about 2 minutes. Season with salt and white pepper. Serve topped with chives. *Serves 6*

COOK'S NOTE: Store bought lobster stock does not taste great in this recipe.

Wine: Chardonnay

Real Maine Lobster Rolls

8   ounces cooked lobster meat, torn into bite-size pieces
3   tablespoons mayonnaise
1   tablespoon butter, room temperature
2   hot dog rolls cut on the top
2   leaves of lettuce, thinly torn

COMBINE lobster meat and mayonnaise in medium bowl. Season to taste with salt. Butter outside surfaces of hot dog rolls. Heat medium skillet over medium-high heat. Place rolls, 1 buttered side down, in skillet; cook until browned slightly, about 2 minutes per side. Open rolls. Fill with lettuce, then lobster mixture, and serve. *Serves 2 girls or one guy (that's just my opinion from up here on the island).*

Grown-Up Mac and Cheese with Maine Lobster

This recipe is so decadent with the combination of cheeses that guests beg for more.

8   ounces tri-color rotini pasta
2   tablespoons salted butter
1   cup whole milk
4   ounces Gruyere cheese, grated
4   ounces Emmentaler cheese, grated
6   ounces shredded sharp cheddar cheese
4   ounces cream cheese
1   pound cooked lobster meat, chopped
1   tablespoon dry sherry
2   tablespoons lobster stock
2   garlic cloves, minced
2   shallots, minced
1   tablespoon olive oil
    salt and pepper to taste

COOK pasta according to instructions, do not overcook.
Melt butter on low heat. Add milk, and cheeses. Heat until blended.
In stockpot heat olive oil, sauté garlic and shallots for 3-4 minutes.

ADD LOBSTER, stock and sherry and sauté until warm, about 2 minutes on low heat. Stir in pasta, mix. Add cheese sauce and serve.
Serves 6

Wine: Puligny-Montrachet, Chappellet Chenin Blanc

Lobster Newberg

3 1½-pound live lobsters
¼ cup unsalted butter
4 tablespoons dry sherry
3 tablespoons cognac or brandy
1 ½ cups heavy cream
¼ teaspoon freshly grated nutmeg
¼ teaspoon cayenne
4 large egg yolks, beaten well
   toast points as an accompaniment

PLUNGE the lobsters into a large kettle of boiling salted water, head first and covered, for 7 minutes from the time the water returns to a boil. Transfer the lobsters with tongs to a cutting board and let them cool until they can be handled. Break off the claws at the body and crack them. Remove the claw meat and cut it into ½-inch pieces. Halve the lobsters length-wise along the undersides, remove the meat from the tails, discarding the bodies, and cut it into ½-inch pieces.

HEAT the lobster meat in the butter over moderate heat, In a heavy saucepan stirring occasionally, for 2 minutes, add 3 tablespoons of the sherry and the brandy, and cook the mixture, stirring, for 2 minutes. Transfer the lobster meat with a slotted spoon to a bowl. Add the cream to the sherry mixture and boil the mixture until it is reduced to about 1 cup. Reduce the heat to low and stir in the remaining 1 teaspoon sherry, the nutmeg, the cayenne, and salt to taste. Whisk in the yolks, cook the mixture, whisking constantly, until it registers 140°F. on a deep-fat thermometer, and cook it, whisking, for 3 minutes more. Stir in the lobster meat and serve the Lobster Newberg over the toast. *Serves 6*

Wine: Muscadet de Sevre et Maine

Asian Lobster Stuffed Sole

Sole is such a mild fish it is fun to be able to pair so many flavors with it.

½   pound lobster meat, chopped
1   egg white
¼   teaspoon minced ginger
2   tablespoons chopped Thai basil
¼   teaspoon Thai chili sauce (*Sambol*)*
1   tablespoon cold diced butter
2   tablespoons lime juice
1   teaspoon sesame oil
¼   cup chopped scallions
1   teaspoon fish sauce
3   tablespoons Panco (*Japanese bread crumbs*)
8   fillets of sole

PREHEAT oven to 375°F. Spray a 9"x 9" baking dish.

PLACE first eight ingredients in food processor and pulse until the consistency of course sausage. Transfer to mixing bowl and fold in scallions, fish sauce, and Japanese bread crumbs.

SPOON 1 tablespoon of stuffing into each fillet of sole and roll. Place in baking dish. Bake uncovered for 15 minutes. *Serves 4*

*****COOK'S NOTE:** *International section of your supermarket.*

Wine: 2004 Maculan Pino & Toi, 2001 Puligny-Montrachet

Baked Maine Lobster Dip

8 ounces low fat cream cheese, room temperature
1 cup cooked Maine lobster meat
1 tablespoon finely chopped onion
2 teaspoons fresh horseradish
½ teaspoon Worcestershire sauce
½ teaspoon Chris's Hot Sauce *(recipe p. 183)*
  milk, as needed to thin *(if desired)*
¼ cup chopped walnuts

SOFTEN the cream cheese, and cut the lobster meat into bite-sized pieces. Stir all the ingredients together, adjusting the consistency with milk, as desired. Place into an oven-proof dish and refrigerate for several hours to meld the flavors. Bake uncovered at 375°F for 25 minutes until bubbly.

Maine Lobster Salad With Spicy Lemon Dressing

¼ cup Meyer lemon juice
2 tablespoons soy sauce
½ teaspoon finely grated garlic
⅛ teaspoon chili paste
¼ teaspoon salt
   freshly ground black pepper to taste
4 tablespoons canola oil

COMBINE all the ingredients except the oil in a jar. When the salt is fully dissolved, add oil. Shake vigorously.

½ pound cooked Maine lobster meat,
   cut in bite-sized pieces
2 tablespoons canola oil for deep-frying garlic
2 elephant cloves garlic, thinly sliced
7 shiitake mushrooms, stems removed
6 ounces baby romaine lettuce
¼ cup Spicy Lemon Dressing

HEAT canola oil in a small saucepan on medium-high. Fry the garlic slices on low until crisp. If you burn garlic it will taste bitter. Drain on paper towel.

LIGHTLY GRILL the mushroom caps.

DIVIDE romaine equally on 4 plates. Arrange mushrooms and lobster on greens. Pour the Spicy Lemon Dressing over all and top with the garlic chips. *Serves 4*

COOK'S NOTE: You can substitute regular lemon and a pinch of sugar for Meyer lemon.

Wine: Chassagne Montrachet, Chardonnay or a light Pinot Noir.

Lobster with Nutmeg Vinaigrette

1 cup chicken stock
1 cup apple cider
4 shallots, minced
1 bay leaf
2 tablespoons sherry vinegar
⅓ cup heavy cream
1 teaspoon freshly grated nutmeg
2 teaspoons canola oil
1 small yellow onion, chopped
1 15-ounce can whole chestnuts
   packed in water, drained
2 tablespoons pure Maine maple syrup
1 tablespoon unsalted butter
¼ cup sour cream
   salt and freshly ground pepper
2 large scallions, chopped
4 1½-pound lobsters, boiled
¼ pound mixed young salad greens

IN A LARGE SAUCEPAN, combine half of the stock with the cider, shallots, bay leaf and sherry vinegar. Boil over high heat until reduced by half, about 25 minutes. Add the heavy cream and nutmeg and simmer over moderate heat until slightly thickened, about 5 minutes. Remove from heat.

HEAT the canola oil in a second saucepan. Add the onion and cook over moderate heat until softened. Add the remaining stock and the chestnuts and simmer until the liquid reduces by a third, about 4 minutes. Remove from the heat and add the maple syrup and butter. Transfer the contents of the saucepan to a blender and puree until smooth. Blend in the sour cream. Transfer the puree to a clean saucepan and season with salt and pepper. Cover and keep warm. Reheat the nutmeg vinaigrette on low. Add the scallions and season with salt and pepper.

CUT the lobster meat into 1-inch chunks. Place mixed greens on four plates. Spoon the chestnut puree on greens. Arrange lobster meat on the puree. Spoon the warm nutmeg vinaigrette over the lobsters and serve at once. *Serves 4*

Lobster Stock

  4   1 ½-pound Maine lobsters
  8   tablespoons *(1 stick)* unsalted butter
  ¼   cup olive oil
  2   medium onions, finely chopped
  2   carrots, peeled and chopped
  2   stalks celery, peeled and chopped
1 ½   teaspoons salt
  2   cups dry white wine
  1   cup Madeira
  5   cups clam juice, or water
  3   cups tomato juice
  1   head garlic, with skins, cut in half horizontally
  ½   bunch fresh parsley, with stems
  1   tablespoon black peppercorns
  2   bay leaves
1 ½   teaspoons dried tarragon
  1   teaspoon dried thyme
  ½   teaspoon cayenne

BRING a large stockpot of water to a rolling boil, add lobsters, and cook at a fast boil until done, about 7 minutes. Transfer to a bowl of iced water to cool, then remove and reserve tail and claw meat for another use. Do this messy job over a bowl to reserve drippings. Crush shells, which will be the base for the stock, using a mallet or hammer, then grind as fine as possible with reserved drippings in a food processor.

MELT butter and oil in a large stockpot over medium-high heat. Cook onions, carrots, celery, and salt until golden, about 10 minutes. Stir in crushed shells, white wine, and Madeira. Turn heat to high and cook until liquid is reduced by half.

ADD clam juice and tomato juice. Bring to a boil and carefully skim and discard foam that rises to surface. Add remaining ingredients and cook at a simmer, uncovered, 1 hour 15 minutes.

STRAIN through a fine sieve and refrigerate up to 2 days or freeze indefinitely.

Simple Maine Lobster Stew

I love to make this a day ahead. Like other leftovers, the flavors are more enhanced.

4 1 ½-pound Maine lobsters
4 tablespoons butter
2 cups lobster stock
1 pint heavy cream
1 quart of milk
  salt and pepper

BOIL the lobsters for 7 minutes. Place cooked lobsters on platters to cool and catch the juices. Pick the meat, reserve the green liver *(tomalley)* and any coral *(roe)*. Set lobster meat aside.

SAUTÉ tomalley and roe in 2 tablespoons of butter in a heavy cooking pot for three minutes. Add half the lobster meat into the pot and sauté for five minutes; repeat this with the rest of the lobster meat. Add the cream, the reserved juice, and the milk.

SIMMER uncovered for 3 hours, do not boil. Add salt and pepper to taste. *Serves 4*

Wine: Korbel Champagne, Brut

Sherry-Ginger Lobster Sauce

Using the best sherry in this recipe makes ALL the difference.

2 cups dry sherry
½ cup lobster stock *(recipe p. 72)*
2 tablespoons honey
7 tablespoons olive oil
½ teaspoon sea salt
½ cup heavy cream
½ teaspoon fresh ginger, minced
1 pound lobster meat, cut in bite-sized pieces

REDUCE sherry over medium heat until ½ cup, about 20 minutes. Add lobster stock and cook 2 more minutes. Add honey and stir to dissolve. Remove from heat. Beat in oil, one tablespoon at a time, as this thickens the sauce. Whip in cream, ginger and salt.

ADD lobster to heat through and serve. *Serves 2.*

Cedar Smoked Salmon

2 salmon fillets
1 ounce light olive oil
  kosher salt
1 teaspoon Sichuan peppercorns *
½ teaspoon salt
½ teaspoon sugar

SPECIAL EQUIPMENT: 1 (½" x 7" x 12") untreated cedar plank, soaked overnight in water.

PREHEAT a grill to high.

DRIZZLE the salmon with just enough oil to coat. Season with salt and pepper. Remove the plank from the water and brush one side with some oil. Place the salmon on plank and sprinkle with pepper mix. Arrange the plank in the middle of the grill so that it smolders on the edges, creating smoke that surrounds the fish. Cook the fish to medium rare, about 6 to 8 minutes, depending upon thickness.

Sichuan peppercorns have a unique woody aroma, pungent citrusy flavor and a tingling numbing effect on the tongue. They are the dried seed of a deciduous prickly ash tree and are not related to true peppercorns. (The Spice House)

COOK'S NOTE: This is great on top of Caesar Salad.

Wine: Pinot Noir or Champagne

Char Provençal

*Artic char is a wonderfully mild fish in the Salmonidae family.
The French influence in this Maine dish is subtle and pleasing.*

1 ½ pounds artic char fillet
1 tablespoon blood orange olive oil
½ cup chopped red onion
2 cups diced tomatoes
¼ cup white wine
½ cup kalamata olives, chopped
1 tablespoon fresh basil, chopped
2 garlic cloves, minced
½ teaspoon lemon thyme, chopped
1 teaspoon sea salt

PREHEAT oven to 375°F.

HEAT oil in sauce pan, add onions and sauté 5 minutes. Add remaining ingredients, except fish and sauté 5 more minutes. Place fish in sprayed 9" x 13" non-stick baking dish. Sprinkle with salt and bake for 10 minutes. Pour sauce over fish and bake 12-15 minutes. *Serves 4*

COOK'S NOTE: You can substitute the blood orange olive oil with 1 tablespoon olive oil and 1/8 teaspoon orange zest.

Wine: Chardonnay (Chateau St. Michelle, CA)

Crab Cakes with Zucchini Tartar Sauce

½ pound crab body meat
1 tablespoon red onion, chopped fine
¼ teaspoon Dijon style mustard
¼ teaspoon Meyer lemon juice, fresh squeezed
¼ teaspoon cayenne
1 medium egg
⅛ teaspoon sweet paprika
½ cup panko crumbs
2 tablespoons olive oil
2 tablespoons salted butter

COMBINE crab meat, onion, mustard, lemon juice, cayenne, egg and paprika. Shape into balls and press to make a small patty. Chill for 1 hour, then roll in panko crumbs.

HEAT the olive oil and butter in cast iron skillet. Cook crab cakes for 2 minutes on each side on medium-high heat. Serve immediately with zucchini tartar sauce.

Zucchini Tartar Sauce

2 tablespoons mayonnaise
1 tablespoon Zucchini Relish *(recipe p. 27)*

MIX and serve with crab cakes.

Downeast Seafood Gumbo

¼ cup olive oil
1 tablespoon Meyer lemon olive oil
1 cup yellow onions, chopped
4 garlic cloves, chopped
3 cups chicken broth
½ cup lobster stock
2 cups plum tomatoes, chopped
2 cups spinach, stems removed, chopped
½ teaspoon cumin, roasted and ground
½ teaspoon cayenne
¼ teaspoon sea salt
½ teaspoon black pepper
1 bay leaf
½ pound cooked Maine shrimp
½ pound cooked mussels *(save half in shells)*
½ pound cooked lobster meat

COOK onions and garlic in oil in a large pot until tender, about 5 minutes.

ADD chicken broth, tomatoes, spinach, cumin, cayenne, salt, pepper and bay leaf. Simmer for 30 minutes. Add shrimp, mussels and lobster just to heat through, about 2 minutes. *Serves 4*

Wine: Red or white burgundy

Maine Seafood Gumbo

I love the combination of spices in this gumbo. The heat helps in the cold winter months up here on the island.

¼ cup olive oil
2 cups yellow onions, chopped
5 garlic cloves, chopped
4 cups chicken broth
½ cup lobster stock *(recipe p. 72, homemade is best but store bought works)*
2 cups plum tomatoes, chopped
½ teaspoon cumin, roasted and ground
½ teaspoon cayenne
⅛ teaspoon salt
½ teaspoon black pepper
2 bay leaves
½ pound cooked Maine shrimp
½ pound Maine crab meat
½ pound cooked Maine lobster meat, cut in chunks

COOK onions and garlic in oil in a large pot until tender, about 5 minutes.

ADD chicken broth, tomatoes, cumin, cayenne, salt, pepper and bay leaves. Simmer for 30 minutes. Add shrimp, crab and lobster just to heat through, about 2 minutes. *Serves 4*

Wine: Louis Jadot Volnay, Chablis

Grilled Halibut Glaze

¼ cup orange juice
¼ cup pineapple
¼ cup papaya
3 tablespoons olive oil
1 tablespoon brown sugar
1 teaspoon orange zest
2 tablespoons chopped, fresh dill
1½ pounds halibut fillet (*1¼ inch thick*)

MIX and marinade fish for at least 1 hour before grilling.

GRILL for 7 minutes on high on one side and 4 minutes on the other side.

Hot and Sweet Grilled Salmon

2 tablespoons Hungarian paprika (*sweet*)
1 teaspoon hot chili powder
¼ teaspoon cayenne pepper
½ teaspoon cumin, roasted and ground
¼ teaspoon sea salt
⅛ teaspoon granulated sugar, ground very fine
3 tablespoons Maine maple syrup
2 pounds salmon fillet

RUB salmon with dry mixture of paprika, chili powder, cayenne, cumin, sea salt and sugar. Place on grill skin side up for 5 minutes, turn over and brush with maple syrup and cook 10 - 15 more minutes, depending on the thickness of the salmon.

COOK'S NOTE: Also great with artic char or halibut. I use freshwater salmon when available.

Layered Maine Shrimp Dish

A crowd pleaser, easy and a great presentation!

8 ounces cream cheese, room temperature
½ cup sour cream
¼ cup mayonnaise
⅛ teaspoon Meyer lemon zest
½ teaspoon fresh dill
8 ounces cooked Maine shrimp
1 cup Downeast Cocktail Sauce (*recipe p. 7*)
2 cups shredded mozzarella cheese
1 yellow pepper, diced
3 scallions (*green and white part*), sliced thin
4 Roma tomatoes, diced

COMBINE cream cheese, sour cream, mayo, zest and dill. Layer on the bottom of 9" x 12" dish. Continue layering, in order, shrimp, cocktail sauce, mozzarella cheese, yellow pepper, scallions and tomatoes. Serve with water crackers, melba or toasted pita.

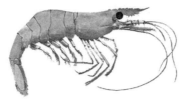

Rocky Coast Clam Chowder

5 cups bottled clam juice
2 tablespoons butter
½ cup yellow onion, finely diced
½ cup sweet onion, finely diced
10 slices cooked bacon, chopped
1 cup flour
8 ounces Maine clams, steamed and chopped
4 medium potatoes, cooked and cut in bite-sized chunks
½ cup milk
½ cup light cream
1 teaspoon salt
¼ teaspoon freshly ground black pepper

HEAT the clam juice in a large saucepan on medium heat. In a separate pan, melt butter and sauté the diced onions until they appear translucent. Add cooked bacon to the onions and stir continuously for 5 minutes. Increase heat on clam juice to medium-high, and with a wire whisk, add flour, then onion and bacon mixture to the liquid. Stir constantly, breaking up any lumps that form.

ADD clams and stir. Add cooked potato chunks, milk, cream, and salt and pepper, continue stirring. Decrease heat to medium-low, and simmer for about 20 minutes, stirring frequently to avoid burning or sticking.

COOK'S NOTE: can substitute six ounces of canned clams, including the juice, if fresh clams not available.

Grilled Swordfish with Mango Salsa

2   10-ounce swordfish steaks
1   ripe mango, peeled and seeded
½   red pepper, chopped
1   fresh jalapeño, seeded and chopped
1   garlic clove, minced
⅓   cup red onion, chopped
¼   cup fresh cilantro, chopped
½   teaspoon lime zest
2   tablespoons fresh lime juice

COMBINE all ingredients except swordfish, toss gently. Grill swordfish, about 6 minutes on each side for a 1½ inch thickness. Serve salsa on top of grilled swordfish.

SALSA can be made up to 6 hours ahead of time. *Serves 4*

Wine: Viognier (Yawmba, South Africa)

Salmon Peppered Jerky

Although I have never been a real jerky fan, this one is a keeper.

2   pounds salmon, skinned and boned
⅔   cup soy sauce
2   tablespoons packed dark brown sugar
1   tablespoon fresh ginger, grated
1   large shallot, minced
1   tablespoon coarse ground Malabar black pepper*

SLICE salmon into ¼ inch-thick strips *(easier when partially frozen)*.

COMBINE all ingredients except salmon and Malabar pepper in a saucepan. Bring to boil, remove from heat. Add salmon and stir to coat, turning a few times gently.

MARINATE salmon for 30 minutes. Place strips on oiled wired racks, such as cookie cooling racks that have been set in cookie pans with sides. Sprinkle salmon with Malabar black pepper. Use more if needed. Let air dry 1 hour.

PLACE pans in 150°F oven until salmon feels firm and leathery, or 4-5 hours. Turn pan every hour for even drying. Cool, store in airtight container or zip-lock plastic bags, and refrigerate.

COOK'S NOTE: I like sockeye salmon for this recipe. I use Malabar Pepper in this recipe to kick up that great pepper taste.

Malabar black pepper is available from The Spice House.

Seafood Fettuccini

This is a delicious, quick and easy recipe. I make my lobster stock ahead and keep plenty in the freezer as it is a time consuming but very rewarding task.

8	ounces fettuccini pasta
1	teaspoon garlic, minced
1	tablespoon extra virgin olive oil
1	cup lobster broth *(recipe p. 72; homemade is best but store bought works)*
1	cup crème fraiche *(combine ½ cup heavy cream and ½ cup sour cream)*
½	cup Maine lobster meat, chopped
½	cup Maine shrimp
½	cup Maine crab meat
¼	cup basil leaves, torn
2	tablespoons fresh chives, chopped

COOK fettuccini until al dente. Toss with fresh garlic and olive oil.

ADD crème fraiche to lobster broth in saucepan and simmer for 3 minutes. Add cooked shrimp, lobster, crab meat and basil and heat through. Pour on top of fettuccini. Sprinkle chives on top and serve. *Serves 4*

Wine: Corton-Charlemagne, or Chablis

Shrimp Jambalaya

2   tablespoons canola oil
1   tablespoon flour
3   tablespoons butter
1   cup finely chopped onion
½   cup finely chopped celery
½   cup finely chopped bell pepper
1 ½   cups lobster stock *(recipe p. 72)*
2   cups water
½   cup finely chopped green onions with tops
1 ¼   cups brown rice
½   cup finely chopped parsley
2   teaspoons salt
½   teaspoon Tellicherry black pepper*
2 ½   cups medium raw shrimp, shelled

MAKE a golden brown roux with oil and flour, set aside. Melt butter in separate large saucepan. Add onion, celery, bell pepper and lobster stock and simmer until almost tender, about ½ hour. Add 2 cups water. Bring to a boil and add green onions, rice, parsley, salt and pepper. Stir to blend and cook covered on low heat for about ½ hour. Add shrimp and roux, cook 8 more minutes. Fluff up rice before serving. *Serves 6*

* *Tellicherry Pepper is available from The Spice House (see Resources).*

Wine: Pine Ridge Chenin Blanc

Steamed Mussels with Harbor Lighthouse Ale

2 pounds mussels, debearded and scrubbed
8 ounces Harbor Lighthouse Ale
½ cup red onion, chopped
1 tablespoon chopped garlic
1 bay leaf
1 tablespoon fresh parsley, chopped for garnish

COMBINE the mussels, ale, onion, garlic, and bay leaf in a large pan. Cover the pan and bring to a boil. Steam until mussels open. Arrange mussels in two bowls.

COOK the liquid until it is reduced by half. Pour the sauce over the mussels.

GARNISH with parsley. *Serves 2*

Wild Game

Bear Bourguignon
Black Bear Casserole
Roasted Cumin Rubbed Bear and Cabernet Glaze
Maine Black Bear Stew
Beaver Baked Beans
Beaver Chili
Beaver Stew with Leeks
Beaver with Tamarind Barbecue Sauce
Curried Goat
Braised Goat Shanks with Orange Zest
Goat Chops with Balsamic Marinade
Thai Goat
Lavender-Marinated Leg of Lamb
Caribbean Lamb
Braised Lamb au Jus Syrah
Maine Moose Stew
Maple Moose Barbecue
Moose and Bar Harbor Stout Chili
Pepperpot Soup
Roasted Walnut and Mushroom Moose Loin
Thai Moose
Venison Chili
Spicy Island Venison
Roasted Venison with Sweet Potatoes and Rosemary Sauce
Venison Stuffed Portobellos
Tarragon and Tomato Rabbit
Braised Rabbit with Fettuccini
Thunder Hole Ale Braised Rabbit

Bear Bourguignon

2   pounds bear, cut into 1-1 ½ inch cubes
2   tablespoons olive oil
2   tablespoons butter
4   carrots, peeled if needed and cut in ½ inch slices
2   cloves garlic, minced
1   large sweet onion, chopped
2   cups beef broth
1   cup dry red wine
2   tablespoons tomato paste
1   teaspoon thyme
    salt and pepper to taste
½   pound fresh button mushrooms, quartered if large
2   tablespoons all-purpose flour
2   tablespoons butter, softened
1   pound egg noodles
2   tablespoons truffle oil

BROWN bear cubes on all sides in oil and butter in a dutch oven on medium-high heat. Add the carrots, onions, garlic, beef broth, wine, tomato paste, thyme, salt and pepper, and mushrooms.

COVER and cook in the oven at 275°F for 6 hours. Remove lid and skim excess fat from surface. On the stovetop, cover and allow to boil lightly.

MIX flour and butter in a bowl until creamy. Add to stew and stir until it is well blended and the stew thickens. Season to taste with salt and pepper and serve on top of noodles with a bit of truffle oil.
Serves 8

SUBSTITUTE CRITTERS: Moose, venison, caribou or elk.

Wine: 1994 Opus One - Meritage

Black Bear Casserole

2   pounds bear meat in 1 inch cubes
½   cup flour
¼   teaspoon nutmeg
½   teaspoon mace
3   tablespoons butter
2   tablespoons blood orange oil *(or canola oil)*
½   pound Crimini mushrooms, quartered
1   14-ounce can diced tomatoes
1   large bay leaf
6   whole allspice berries
1   cup Cabernet Sauvignon wine
½   cup heavy cream

PREHEAT oven to 350°F.

MIX nutmeg, mace and flour in a bag and add bear. Dredge bear cubes. Heat butter and oil in heavy skillet and brown meat on medium high. Add tomatoes and mushrooms, and cook covered for 5 minutes.

TRANSFER to 4 quart casserole and add bay leaf, allspice and wine. Cover and bake 1½ hours. Stir in cream, bake 10 minutes more. Serve over rice or noodles. *Serves 4*

SUBSTITUTE CRITTERS: Lamb, moose, venison or caribou.

Wine: 1996 Reserve Chateau Rayas Chateauneuf-du-Pape

Roasted Cumin Rubbed Bear and Cabernet Glaze

4   lean and thin bear steaks, 10 ounces each
     salt and pepper for seasoning steaks
2   tablespoons vegetable oil
2   tablespoons butter
     Roasted Cumin Rub *(see recipe on opposite page)*
½   cup minced shallots
1   tablespoon minced garlic
1   cup red wine *(Cabernet Sauvignon-like)*
⅓   cup chives, chopped *(for garnish)*

PREHEAT oven to 200°F and heat a plate.

SEASON bear with salt and pepper. In a cast iron skillet, heat oil over medium-high heat, heavily sear bear on both sides, about 2 minutes. Place cooked bear on warmed plate from oven while cooking the rest of the steaks. Rub cumin rub on all cooked steaks, let sit.

SAUTÉ shallots and garlic in same skillet for 2 minutes. Add wine and deglaze, about 7 minutes. Return bear back to pan to heat through. Place steaks on plates and cover with sauce. Great with garlic mashed potatoes and steamed broccoli. *Serves 4*

SUBSTITUTE CRITTERS: Venison, moose, caribou or elk.

Roasted Cumin Rub

¼ cup roasted cumin
¼ cup roasted coriander
2 tablespoons ground black pepper
½ cup dark brown sugar
2 tablespoons minced garlic
3 tablespoons minced shallots
1 tablespoon sea salt

ROAST cumin and coriander, separately in cast iron pan. Cool, then grind.

MIX all ingredients together. Store in glass jar.

Wine: 1996 Stag's Leap Cabernet Sauvignon

Maine Black Bear Stew

⅓ cup flour
½ teaspoon salt
½ teaspoon pepper
1 tablespoon oregano
1 tablespoon bacon grease
4 tablespoons unsalted butter
2 pounds cubed black bear
3 large carrots, sliced
¼ cup red onion, chopped
½ cup yellow onion, chopped
1 tablespoon toasted celery seed
4 garlic cloves, minced
2 ½ cups Cabernet Sauvignon
2 large Maine potatoes, peeled and chopped
½ pound Portobello mushrooms, sliced
1 tablespoon dried rosemary
3 sprigs fresh rosemary
2 bay leaves
2 cups beef stock
1 cup mushroom stock

COMBINE flour, salt, pepper, and oregano in a plastic bag. Shake. Dredge bear meat in mixture.

HEAT bacon grease and butter in a large stockpot over moderate-high heat until somewhat browned. Add carrots, onions, celery seed, garlic, and cook for 5 minutes. Add remainder of ingredients except stock. Deglaze wine for 1 hour, simmering uncovered. Add stock and simmer 1 hour, sauce will thicken. Season with more salt and pepper, if necessary. Stir stew to avoid scorching. *Serves 6*

SUBSTITUTE CRITTERS: Moose or venison.

Wine: Zinfandel, Cabernet or Bordeaux

Beaver Baked Beans

1	pound dry Great Northern beans
8	cups boiling water
2	beaver legs
1	medium yellow onion, skinned
2	large carrots, cut in 2 inch slices
½	pound button mushrooms, cleaned
½	cup dark brown sugar
1	teaspoon dry mustard
1	tablespoon cranberry mustard
½	teaspoon salt
½	teaspoon black pepper
½	cup molasses

SOAK beans overnight. Strain and rinse in the morning.
Boil water.

IN a 2 pound bean pot place in order, beaver legs, whole onion, carrots, mushrooms, beans, sugar, mustards, salt, pepper, molasses then boiling water. (You may not need all 8 cups). Pour water over the beans, enough to cover an inch above the beans.

BAKE at a 300°F oven for 6-8 hours. Keep checking them after 4 hours to make sure there is enough water in the beanpot.

Beaver Chili

½ pound bacon
3 pounds beaver in 1 inch cubes
2 tablespoons cayenne pepper
2 tablespoons Mexican oregano
1 tablespoon roasted, ground cumin
1 tablespoon sea salt
1 tablespoon minced garlic
½ cup water
1 large yellow onion, chopped
1 large sweet onion, chopped

96

COOK bacon in a 3 quart stockpot. Place cooked bacon on paper towel, reserve for another use. Brown the beaver cubes in bacon fat until well browned. Pour off extra fat, if any (beaver is very lean and I rarely have fat left over).

COMBINE meat and all spices in Dutch oven, mix to coat meat thoroughly. Return to heat, add ½ cup water and cook 10 minutes. Add onions and simmer for one hour. If you need more moisture, add water.

SUBSTITUTE CRITTERS: Elk, caribou, venison or moose.

Wine: Cabernet Sauvignon (Penfolds, S.E. Australia)

Beaver Stew with Leeks

2 pounds boneless beaver leg meat,
  trimmed of excess fat, cut into 2 inch pieces
1 cup chopped fresh Italian parsley
3 garlic cloves, minced
1 tablespoon finely grated lemon zest
3 tablespoons olive oil
2 large leeks *(white and pale green parts only)*,
  thinly sliced, about 2 ½ cups
1 large onion, thinly sliced
¾ teaspoon dried thyme
1 ½ cups *(or more)* low-salt chicken broth

PLACE trimmed beaver in large bowl; sprinkle generously with salt and pepper. Cover and let stand at room temperature 30 minutes.

COMBINE ¾ cup parsley, garlic, and lemon zest in small bowl. Reserve remaining ¼ cup parsley for garnish. Heat oil in heavy large pot over high heat. Working in batches, add beaver and cook until well browned on all sides, about 7 minutes per batch. Transfer to medium bowl. Add leeks and onion to drippings in pot and sauté until softened, about 7 minutes. Add chopped parsley mixture and thyme; stir 30 seconds. Return beaver and any accumulated juices to pot. Add broth and bring to boil. Reduce heat to medium-low; cover and simmer until beaver is very tender, about 1 ½ hours. *Serves 4*

SUBSTITUTE CRITTERS: Lamb, moose, venison, or caribou.

Wine: 1986 Chateau Haut Brion or Ridge Zinfandel Sonoma Station

Beaver with Tamarind Barbecue Sauce

1 pound beaver, cut into 1 inch cubes

1 tablespoon ground coriander

½ teaspoon salt

1¼ teaspoons freshly ground pepper

2 tablespoons blood orange olive oil

½ cup tamarind concentrate

⅓ cup light brown sugar

2 tablespoons soy sauce

1½ tablespoons molasses

2 garlic cloves, minced

¼ cup canola oil

6 large shallots, thinly sliced

MARINATE beaver in a medium shallow glass baking dish, sprinkle with coriander, salt and 1 teaspoon pepper. Add olive oil and toss to coat. Let marinate for 30 minutes.

IN A MEDIUM SAUCEPAN, combine the tamarind, sugar, soy sauce, molasses, garlic and the remaining coriander and pepper. Bring to a boil, then simmer over moderate heat, uncovered, for 5 minutes. Let cool.

HEAT canola oil in a deep skillet until shimmering. Add the shallots and fry over moderate heat, stirring, until golden and crisp, 5 minutes. With a slotted spoon, transfer to paper towels. Add beaver to remaining oil and sear on high, stirring constantly, for 10 minutes.

ADD tamarind barbecue sauce and simmer for 25 minutes. Spoon on top of buttered noodles and top with fried shallots.
Serves 4

Wine: Cabernet Sauvignon - Tempranillo

Curried Goat

6 pounds goat stew meat, shoulder
   cut into 1 ½ inch pieces
4 cups sliced onions
1 large tomato, seeded and chopped
2 tablespoons chopped fresh ginger
6 garlic cloves, crushed
6 tablespoons Maharajah curry powder*
   salt and freshly ground pepper
2 tablespoons ghee* or vegetable oil
1 tablespoon Chris's Hot Sauce *(recipe p. 183)*
¼ cup water
4 Maine potatoes, peeled and diced
1 bunch scallions, thinly sliced for garnish

IN A LARGE BOWL, season goat meat with onions, tomato, ginger, garlic, curry powder, salt, and pepper. Mix well and marinate in the refrigerator, overnight.

PREHEAT the oven to 375°F.

REMOVE meat from marinade. In a large stainless stockpot, over a moderately high heat, brown off the meat in ghee or oil until golden brown on all sides. Add the reserved marinade and hot sauce and sauté for 6 minutes. Return meat to pot with enough water to just cover the meat and bring to a boil. Cover and put pot in the oven for 1 ½ hours. Add the potatoes to the pot, return the pot to the oven and cook for another ½ hour, or until meat is tender. *Serves 8*

*COOK'S NOTE: Maharajah curry powder is available from The Spice House (see Resources). Ghee is a solid clarified butter,

SUBSTITUTIONS: Venison, pork, beef or lamb.

Wine: Bordeaux or Cabernet

Braised Goat Shanks with Orange Zest

4 meaty 1-pound goat shanks, trimmed
    kosher salt and freshly ground pepper
2 tablespoons blood orange olive oil
1 carrot, coarsely chopped
1 small onion, coarsely chopped
2 cups dry red wine
2 14.5-ounce cans Italian peeled tomatoes
    with their juice
2 cups chicken stock
10 garlic cloves, peeled
2 bay leaves
1 cinnamon stick
4 sprigs fresh parsley tied together or
    1 tablespoon dried parsley

Garnish:

1 tablespoon minced fresh parsley
2 teaspoons grated orange zest
1 garlic clove, minced

PREHEAT the oven to 325°F.

SEASON the goat shanks generously with salt and pepper. Heat the blood orange olive oil in a large stockpot. Working in batches, brown the goat shanks thoroughly over moderately high heat, turning often, about 3 minutes per side; transfer the shanks to a large bowl. Add one tablespoon olive oil and the carrots and onion and cook, over moderately high heat, stirring occasionally until browned, about 5 minutes. Add the wine and boil for 5 minutes, using a wooden spoon to scrape up the browned bits from the bottom of the pot. Return the goat to the casserole. Add the tomatoes, chicken stock, whole garlic cloves, the bay leaves and cinnamon stick. Tie the parsley sprigs with string and add them to the pot. Bring to a boil, then cover and cook in the preheated oven for 1 ½ hours.

REMOVE the pot from the oven. Transfer the goat shanks to a large bowl and cover with foil. Pick out and discard the cinnamon sticks, bay leaves and parsley. Let the cooking liquid stand for 5 minutes, and then skim off the fat. Puree the cooking liquid and vegetables in a blender or in the pot with an immerser. Pour the sauce back into the casserole. Boil the sauce until reduced by half, stirring frequently, about 30 minutes. Season with salt and pepper and return the goat shanks to the sauce. Bring the shanks to a simmer. In a small bowl, combine the minced garlic with the minced parsley and orange zest. Set a goat shank on each plate. Spoon the sauce over the meat, sprinkle with the zest and serve. Great with mashed carrots and turnips salted and buttered, and long grain white rice. *Serves 4*

Wine: 1996 Wente Reliz Creek Reserve Pinot Noir

Goat Chops with Balsamic Marinade

The combination of the marinade and the chewy red wine sauce on the goat keeps the palate screaming for more.

⅓ cup balsamic vinegar
⅓ cup soy sauce
¼ teaspoon Chris's Hot Sauce *(recipe p. 183)*
1 tablespoon finely grated orange zest
8 two-inch goat chops
  salt and freshly ground pepper
½ cup blood orange olive oil *(vegetable oil)*
½ cup red wine *(zinfandel or other red wine you are drinking with this dish)*
¼ cup balsamic vinegar

PREHEAT the oven to 450°F.

COMBINE the vinegar, soy sauce, hot sauce and orange zest in a bowl. Add the goat and marinate at room temperature for 2 hours, turning once. Remove the goat from the marinade and pat dry, reserve marinade. Season the goat with salt and pepper. In large skillet, heat oil until shimmering. Add the goat and sear over moderately high heat until nicely browned, about 3 minutes on each side. Transfer goat to a rimmed baking sheet. Roast in the upper third of the oven for 15 minutes. Let the goat rest for 10 minutes before serving on warmed plate.

ADD wine and vinegar to marinade in skillet, reduce 5 minutes. Pour over goat. *Serves 8*

SUBSTITUTE CRITTERS: Lamb, venison, moose or pork.

Wine: 2003 Brown Estate Red Zinfandel

Thai Goat

¼ cup canola oil
1 yellow onion, chopped
2 garlic cloves, minced
1 cup coconut milk
2 tablespoons curry paste
2 teaspoons fish sauce
½ teaspoon palm sugar
1 pound lean goat meat, cubed
4 teaspoons lime zest
25 Thai basil leaves

HEAT canola oil on medium in wok. Stir in onion and garlic until browned. Add coconut milk, curry paste, fish sauce and sugar, cook 2 minutes. Add goat and cook 20 minutes on medium. Stir in lime zest and basil leaves and serve. Add a little water if necessary but finished dish should be dry. Serve over rice noodles. *Serves 4*

Wine: White Rioja, Alsatian wine

Lavender-Marinated Leg of Lamb

1   5-pound butterflied leg of lamb, trimmed
4   anchovy fillets, cut crosswise into 24 pieces
2   garlic cloves, each cut into 6 slices and
    halved lengthwise
2   teaspoons rosemary, minced
¼   cup extra-virgin olive oil, plus more for serving
½   cup dry white wine (*such as Pinot Blanc*)
1   tablespoon dried lavender
½   teaspoon sea salt
½   teaspoon freshly ground pepper

USING a small sharp knife, make 24 incisions all over the lamb. Stuff each incision with a piece of anchovy and garlic and a pinch of the rosemary. In a roasting pan, combine the ¼ cup of olive oil with the wine and lavender. Add the lamb and coat well. Cover and refrigerate overnight.

LIGHT a grill. Bring the lamb to room temperature and season with salt and pepper. Grill the lamb over a moderately low fire for about 40 minutes, or until lightly charred and an instant-read thermometer inserted in the thickest part registers 125°F for medium rare. Transfer the lamb to a carving board, cover with foil and let rest for 10 minutes before thinly slicing it. Serve with sea salt and olive oil roasted tomato halves. *Serves: 8*

SUBSTITUTE CRITTERS: Moose, venison, caribou or elk.

COOK'S NOTE: Butterfly the lamb so it's about the same thickness all over and will cook evenly on the grill.

Wine: 1996 Dominus; Bordeaux-style wine enhances the earthiness of the lamb, and allows the lavender through without overpowering it.

Caribbean Lamb

- 1 cup curry powder
- 3 large sprigs thyme
- 3 scotch bonnet peppers, finely chopped
  (*or jalapeño peppers*)
- 2 onions, diced
- 1 bunch scallions, diced
  (*reserve some greens for garnish*)
  salt and freshly ground black pepper
- ¼ cup canola oil
- ½ cup chopped fresh garlic
- 4 pounds lamb roast, bone in
- 1 carrot, diced
- 2 tomatoes, diced
- 1 pound potatoes, diced
- ½ cup fresh ginger, chopped
- 3 quarts chicken stock

TO MAKE THE MARINADE, combine curry, thyme, scotch bonnets, onions, scallions, salt and pepper. Marinate the lamb meat overnight. Remove the lamb from the marinade, reserve leftover marinade.

HEAT oil on high in a large cast iron pan, add garlic and sear the lamb roast on all sides. Add reserved marinade, carrots, tomatoes, potatoes and ginger. Add stock and stew for approximately 1 hour until meat is tender or about to fall off the bone.

REMOVE the meat from the pot, place on a platter and cover with aluminum foil. Return the pan to the stove over medium heat and cook until sauce is thickened. Season with salt and additional hot sauce, if desired. Garnish meat with scallions. *Serves 8*

SUBSTITUTE CRITTERS: Goat or venison.

Wine: Cabernet Sauvignon or Bordeaux

Braised Lamb au Jus Syrah

6   1-pound lamb shanks
½   teaspoon each salt and freshly ground pepper
¼   cup olive oil
3   medium carrots, coarsely chopped
2   celery ribs, coarsely chopped
2   small, yellow onions, coarsely chopped
1   tablespoon tomato paste
2   cups Cabernet Sauvignon or other hearty red wine
1   bay leaf
6   whole Malabar black peppercorns*
4   cups chicken stock
1   cup (packed) flat-leaf parsley leaves, finely chopped
2   teaspoons finely grated lemon zest
4   garlic cloves, minced

PREHEAT oven to 300°F. Season the lamb shanks with salt and pepper. Heat ¼ cup of the olive oil in a large enameled cast-iron casserole. Working in batches, cook the lamb shanks over moderate heat, turning often, until well browned on all sides, about 12 minutes; transfer to a platter.

ADD the carrots, celery and onions and cook over moderate heat until the vegetables start to brown, about 8 minutes. Stir in the tomato paste, and then add the wine, scraping up the browned bits from the bottom. Stir in the bay leaf and peppercorns. Return the lamb shanks to the casserole and add the stock. Bring to a boil, cover and bake the shanks in the oven for about 3 hours, or until the meat is very tender. Transfer the shanks to the platter and remove the meat from the bones. Put the meat in a bowl and cover with a damp towel.

STRAIN the sauce into a large saucepan, pressing on the vegetables to extract as much liquid as possible. Boil the sauce over high heat until it is thick enough to coat the back of a spoon, about 25 minutes; season with salt and pepper. Return the lamb to the sauce and rewarm over moderate heat. In a small bowl, mix the parsley with the lemon zest and garlic. Spoon the lamb stew over rice or risotto, sprinkle with zest and serve.

Malabar black peppercorns available from The Spice House - see Resources

Wine: Cabernet Sauvignon or Bordeaux

Maine Moose Stew

2 tablespoons porcini olive oil (*or canola oil*)
2 tablespoons butter
1½ pounds moose meat, cubed
2 tablespoons Bouquet Garni (*recipe p. 182*)
½ teaspoon salt
¼ teaspoon jerk seasoning (*dry or wet seasoning works*)
1 cup dry vermouth
2 cups Vidalia onions, chopped in chunks
1 cup shiitake mushrooms
1 cup button mushrooms
1 cup sweet pepper, chopped (*yellow preferred*)
2 tablespoons crushed garlic
1½ cups diced tomatoes (*or 1 can*)
2 cups beef broth
salt and pepper

HEAT oil and butter in a large stockpot over moderate-high heat until somewhat browned.

ADD moose and brown on all sides. Add remainder of ingredients (except tomatoes and broth). Simmer about 10 minutes. Add tomatoes and broth and simmer 1 hour, covered. Stir stew often to avoid scorching. Season with salt and pepper to taste. *Serves 4*

SUBSTITUTE CRITTERS: Venison, elk, caribou, goat, buffalo, or beef.

Wine: Chateau Montelena Cabernet Sauvignon, or a Rhone-like wine

Maple Moose Barbecue

- 4   1 ½ inch thick moose steaks
- 2   tablespoons canola oil
- ¾   cup Maine maple syrup
- 2   tablespoons chopped chipotle peppers
- 2   tablespoons apple cider vinegar
- 2   tablespoons onion, minced
- 1   tablespoon Worcestershire sauce
- 1   teaspoon kosher salt
- ½   teaspoon hot dry mustard
- ½   teaspoon ground black pepper

PREHEAT oven to 375°F.

COMBINE all ingredients except oil and moose. Marinate steaks for one hour in barbecue marinade, turning once.

HEAT oil in cast-iron skillet on high. Sear steaks, 2 minutes on each side. Baste with marinade on both sides then place skillet in oven to finish for 10 minutes. Let rest 3 minutes before serving, which keeps the juices intact. *Serves 4*

SUBSTITUTE CRITTERS: Venison.

Wine: Bordeaux (such as Côtes du Roussillon Villages Chateau Triniau)

Moose and Bar Harbor Stout Chili

This dish is perfect after a day of ice fishing;
it really sticks to your bones.

1	tablespoon roasted, ground cumin
2	teaspoons roasted, ground coriander
3	pounds ground moose
2	tablespoons canola oil
1 ½	pounds onions, coarsely chopped
1	pound red bell peppers, seeded, cut into ½-inch pieces
1	pound yellow bell peppers, seeded, cut into ½-inch pieces
2	large jalapeño chilies with seeds, chopped, about ⅓ cup
4	tablespoons chili powder
4	cups crushed tomatoes, not drained
2	15-ounce cans kidney beans, drained
1	12-ounce bottle Bar Harbor Stout
	sour cream
	chopped green onions
	coarsely grated extra-sharp cheddar cheese

ROAST cumin and coriander, separately, in cast-iron skillet over medium heat until dark and beginning to smoke, about 4 minutes. Stir constantly. Cool and grind.

SAUTÉ moose in heavy large pot over medium-high heat until no longer pink, about 8 minutes. Heat oil in another large skillet over medium-high heat. Add onions, bell peppers, and jalapeños. Sauté until vegetables begin to soften, about 15 minutes. Add mixture to pot with moose. Mix in toasted spices and chili powder. Add crushed tomatoes, beans, and stout. Bring chili to boil, stirring occasionally. Reduce heat and simmer 20 minutes, stirring often. Season with salt and pepper. *Serves 8*

LADLE chili into bowls. Serve with sour cream, green onions, and cheese.

SUBSTITUTE CRITTERS: Venison, bear or beaver.

Wine: Merlot or Cabernet Sauvignon

Pepperpot Soup

Simple and delicious!

1   cup beef bouillon
8   ounces ox tail
8   ounces stew beef
1   cup chopped spinach
1   cup Indian kale
1   dozen okras, pureed
2   cups coconut milk
2   yams, peeled and chopped
1   jalapeño, deseeded and chopped
1   tablespoon brown sugar
½   teaspoon nutmeg
3   scallions, white part chopped

SIMMER ox tail and stew beef in bouillon until meat tender, about 30 minutes. Debone ox tail and return meat back to soup. Add rest of ingredients and simmer 2 more hours.

Roasted Walnut and Mushroom Moose Loin

6   tablespoons unsalted butter
3   tablespoons roasted walnut oil
4   7-ounce boneless moose loins, about 2 inches thick
4   large shallots, chopped
4   cloves minced garlic
8   ounces Crimini mushrooms (a.k.a. baby Portobellos), quartered
1   cup dry white wine
1   cup game stock, or ½ cup beef stock and ½ cup mushroom stock
1   tablespoon tomato paste
1   tablespoon beurre manié*
2   tablespoons minced Italian flat parsley
4   large garlic toasts *(1 for each loin)*

HEAT half butter and oil on high heat in skillet. Sear all loins on both sides, about 3 minutes each. Remove onto warm dish.

SAUTÉ remaining butter, shallots, and mushrooms, about 5 minutes. Add wine and boil. Reduce the liquid by ¾. Add stock and tomato paste, mix well. Stir in beurre manié and simmer 5 minutes.

RETURN loins to pan and turn to thoroughly coat. Serve on garlic toast and sprinkle parsley on top. *Serves 4*

SUBSTITUTE CRITTERS: Lamb, venison, bear, caribou or elk.

*COOK'S NOTE: Beurre manié: combine equal parts flour and soft butter, for thickening.

Wine: 1986 Chateau Haut Brion, Cabernet Sauvignon or similar

Thai Moose

4 moose steaks
1 tablespoon tamarind paste
1 tablespoon garlic, chopped
1 tablespoon fresh ginger, chopped
¼ cup Thai curry paste *(red)*
½ cup hoisin sauce
¼ cup soy sauce
¼ cup balsamic vinegar
1 tablespoon dark sesame oil
½ cup chicken stock

COMBINE all ingredients, except moose, to make sauce. Marinade the moose steaks for one hour, turning once. Grill moose steaks on medium-high heat, basting at each turn with sauce (about 6 to 8 minutes depending on the thickness and desired rareness of the steak).

SERVE on a bed of rasmine rice cooked in chicken stock. *Serves 4*

SUBSTITUTIONS: Venison, bear, elk, caribou or beef.

Wine: 1991 Ridge Zinfandel Sonoma Station; Sangiovese

Venison Chili

4 tablespoons vegetable oil
3 pounds ground venison
3 medium yellow onions, chopped
5 tablespoons fresh, minced garlic
¼ cup chili powder
2 teaspoons roasted, ground cumin
3 tablespoons sweet paprika
3 cups beef stock
½ cup red wine (*Cabernet Sauvignon*)
4 14.5-ounce cans diced tomatoes
4 yellow peppers, diced
2 cans red kidney beans, drained
3 tablespoons tomato paste

HEAT oil in large pot over medium high heat, add onions and cook until tender. Add garlic, chili, cumin and paprika and cook 3 minutes. Add ground venison and cook 10 minutes, stir until all venison is broken up. Add stock, wine and tomatoes and bring to a boil. Lower heat and simmer covered for 45 minutes. Add peppers, beans and tomato paste.

SIMMER uncovered for 25 more minutes.

TOP with grated cheddar or a dollop of sour cream.

SUBSTITUTE CRITTERS: Moose, caribou, elk or beef.

Beer: Dark beer or stout

Spicy Island Venison

2 pounds venison stew meat
1 lime, juiced
1 tablespoon salt
1 teaspoon freshly ground black pepper
1 Scotch bonnet pepper, seeded and minced
½ teaspoon dried thyme
½ teaspoon ground allspice *(dried pimento berries)*
3 tablespoons curry powder
2 whole scallions, sliced
1 onion, sliced
3 cloves garlic, minced
¼ cup garlic olive oil
3 tomatoes, diced
½ cup coconut milk
7 cups water

RINSE meat well, rub lime juice over venison. Place meat in a bowl, then add salt, black pepper, Scotch bonnet, thyme, allspice, curry powder, scallions, onion and garlic. Marinate for 5 hours in the refrigerator.

HEAT the oil in a skillet until it is very hot and sauté the meat until golden brown. Then add the marinade, tomatoes and coconut milk, and simmer for approximately 3 more minutes. Add water, reduce heat and allow to simmer for 2 to 3 hours stirring occasionally until meat is tender.

SUBSTITUTE CRITTERS: Moose, caribou, bear or elk.

Wine: David Arthur Cabernet Sauvignon, Chateau de Beaucastel Chateauneuf-du-Pape

Roasted Venison with Sweet Potatoes and Rosemary Sauce

I first made this recipe with fried potatoes. Dan suggested baking them, and I love the flavor change!

1 ¼	cup extra-virgin olive oil
½	cup rosemary leaves, finely chopped
1	head of garlic, minced
	finely grated zest of 1 lemon
¼	cup fresh lemon juice
½	teaspoon crushed red pepper flakes
	kosher salt
1	5-pound boneless venison roast, butterflied
	freshly ground black pepper
1	stick unsalted butter
5	large sweet potatoes, peeled and sliced ¼ inch thick
2	tablespoons olive oil

PREHEAT the oven to 500°F.

COMBINE the oil, rosemary, garlic, lemon zest, lemon juice, crushed red pepper and 1 tablespoon kosher salt. *(This sauce is best made 2 days ahead and refrigerated).*

SEASON the venison with salt and pepper and brush ½ cup of rosemary sauce on both sides. Set the venison aside, fat side up, on a large rimmed baking sheet and roast in the upper third of the oven for about 25 minutes, or until an instant-read thermometer inserted in the thickest part of the meat registers 130°F for medium rare. Transfer the venison to a cutting board, cover with foil and let rest for 10 minutes.

TOSS the potatoes in ⅓ cup rosemary sauce. Transfer the potatoes to a baking sheet and season with salt. Bake for 25 minutes, turning once. Reheat the sauce and thickly slice the venison. Arrange the potatoes on a plate and top with the venison and spoon remaining warm sauce over it all. *Serves: 6*

SUBSTITUTE CRITTERS: Moose, bear, elk, caribou or beef.

Wine: Merlot, Cabernet Franc

Venison Stuffed Portobellos

4 large Portobello mushrooms
½ cup heavy cream
1 tablespoon dry mustard seed
1 pound ground venison meat
1 medium yellow onion
2 teaspoons minced fresh garlic
3 teaspoons Dijon style mustard
½ teaspoon ground rosemary
½ teaspoon English thyme
1 large egg

PREHEAT oven to 350°F.

CLEAN mushrooms, spray both sides with cooking spray *(I like olive oil)*. Bring to boil cream and dry mustard seeds. Simmer 5 minutes, let cool.

COMBINE all other ingredients in a large bowl. Make 4 patties, then place patties on top of mushrooms. Place on baking sheet and cover with aluminum foil.

BAKE for 35 minutes. Serve immediately with mustard sauce.

SUBSTITUTE CRITTERS: Moose, lamb or beef.

Tarragon and Tomato Rabbit

- 4 tablespoons olive oil
- 2 tablespoons unsalted butter
- 2 rabbits, cut into serving pieces
  salt and pepper
- 2 onions, cut into large chunks
- 5 garlic cloves, chopped
- 4 carrots, chopped *(2 yellow and 2 orange)*
- 1 cup tarragon vinegar
- 2 pounds ripe tomatoes, seeded and chopped
- 2 cups dry white wine *(Pouilly-Fuissé)*
- 2 tablespoons dried tarragon
- 1 teaspoon dried thyme
- ¼ cup chicken stock
- ½ teaspoon ground Lampong black pepper*
- ¼ cup tomato paste

HEAT oil and butter in large, deep skillet. Salt and pepper the rabbit. Lay the rabbit, skin side down in the oil and brown for 3 to 4 minutes on each side. Remove the rabbit from the pan and set aside.

SAUTÉ onions until tender. Add the remaining ingredients, except tomato paste. Bring the liquid up to a simmer and cook for 15 minutes. Stir tomato paste into vegetable mixture. Add the rabbit back to the pan and continue to simmer for 20 minutes. Serve the rabbit on top of noodles lightly tossed with butter. *Serves 6*

SUBSTITUTE CRITTERS: Chicken or turkey

*Lampong is a spicy black pepper available from The Spice House.

Wine: Shiraz (Shottesbrooke, Australia)

Braised Rabbit with Fettuccini

1   3-pound rabbit, cut into 8 serving pieces
½   teaspoon salt
¼   teaspoon black pepper
¼   cup extra-virgin olive oil
2   medium onions, halved and cut into ¼-inch slices
4   garlic cloves, finely chopped
2   strips fresh orange zest
1   4-inch cinnamon stick
2   Turkish bay leaves
½   cup dry red wine
2   cups canned crushed tomatoes
½   cup water
     salt and pepper to taste
8   ounces fettuccine
1   tablespoon chopped fresh flat-leaf parsley *(garnish)*

PREHEAT oven to 350°F.

DRY rabbit pieces and sprinkle with salt and pepper. Heat 2 tablespoons oil in skillet over moderately high heat until hot but not smoking, then brown rabbit in 2 batches, turning over once, about 6 minutes per batch. Transfer to warm plate.

REDUCE heat to medium and cook onions, garlic, zest, cinnamon stick, and bay leaves in remaining 2 tablespoons oil, stirring frequently, for 5 minutes. Add wine and deglaze skillet by boiling, scraping up any brown bits, until wine is reduced by half, about 2 minutes. Stir in tomatoes and water. Place rabbit back in sauce and bring to a simmer.

COVER skillet tightly with lid or heavy-duty foil, then braise in middle of oven 30 minutes. Turn rabbit over and continue to braise, covered, until rabbit is tender, 25 to 30 minutes more. Cook pasta in a large pot of boiling salted water, while rabbit is braising. Drain pasta well in a colander and transfer to a large platter. Discard zest, cinnamon stick, and bay leaf from sauce. Arrange rabbit over pasta, then spoon sauce over top and sprinkle with parsley. *Serves 4*

Wine: Merlot, Zinfandel (St. Francis, Sonoma)

Thunder Hole Ale Braised Rabbit

3 tablespoons olive oil
2 whole rabbits, skin on and cut into individual pieces
½ teaspoon garlic salt
½ cup flour
½ pound bacon
2 cups thinly sliced red onions
1½ pounds pearl oyster mushrooms, thinly sliced
3 tablespoons chopped garlic
1 tablespoon chopped fresh thyme
2 bay leaves
2 cups Thunder Hole Ale *(or other amber beer)*
2 cups chicken stock
1 cup mushroom stock
2 tablespoons butter
2 tablespoons flour
  salt and ground pepper to taste
1 tablespoon parsley, finely chopped

HEAT oil in a large, oven-proof pan with a lid. Salt and pepper the rabbit. Mix ½ cup flour with garlic salt. Dredge the rabbit pieces in the seasoned flour, coating each side completely. Lay the rabbit, skin side down in the oil and brown for 3 to 4 minutes on each side. Remove the rabbit from the pan and set aside.

COOK bacon and add the onions. Season with salt and pepper, sauté for 2 to 3 minutes or until tender.

ADD the mushrooms and garlic and sauté for 2 minutes. Add thyme, bay leaves and rabbit to the vegetable mixture. Add the ale and stock. Bring the liquid up to a simmer and cover. Cook the rabbit until tender, about 30 minutes, skimming off the fat.

REMOVE the rabbit pieces from the pan and set aside. Blend the 2 tablespoons flour and butter together into a smooth paste. Whisk the paste into the hot liquid. Bring the liquid to a simmer and cook for 3 to 4 minutes. Add the rabbit back to the pan and continue to cook for 5 minutes. Stir in the parsley. Serve the rabbit over chunked sweet potato.

COOK'S NOTE: shiitake or button mushrooms can be substituted for the pearl oyster mushrooms, but the pearl oysters are worth looking for.

Wine: Merlot (Duckhorn)

Birds

8 O'Clock Bird
Autumn Chicken
Chicken Divan
Chicken Tortilla Soup for the Soulmate
Garlic-Rosemary Chicken
Gingered Turkey Noodle Soup
Grilled Chicken Marsala
Grilled Beer Can Chicken
Southwest Harbor Turkey Chili
Mustard-Thyme Chicken Breast
Wild Pan-Asian Turkey Loaf
Partridge with Apple Cider Glaze
Pheasant with Shiitake Mushrooms
Rosemary Citrus Chicken
Seared Chicken and Sun-Dried Tomatoes
on Angel Hair
Smoked Duck in Raspberry Sauce
Smoked Wild Goose
Tarragon and Tomato Partridge
Marinated Wild Turkey Breast
Smoked Turkey Soup

125

8 O'Clock Bird

a.k.a. Parmesan Crusted Wild Turkey with Sage Pepper Sauce.
My girlfriend, Kat, was hunting turkeys one day when she saw one
across the river. The river was too deep to venture across. While she
was debating what to do, the bird took off and headed straight
towards her. In shock she watched it fly directly at her, and she
finally lifted her gun only to be winged in the head as it flew off.
The next time she saw this crazed turkey, at 8 O'Clock, she shot
and swam. This recipe was created especially for Kat and her bird!

4	large wild turkey cutlets, ¾ inch cut from the breast
1	large egg
1	egg white
1	cup finely grated fresh Parmesan
½	teaspoon garlic powder
½	teaspoon lemon zest
2	cups panko crumbs
½	teaspoon salt
2	tablespoons Meyer lemon olive oil
3	tablespoons butter

PREHEAT oven to 450°F.

BLEND eggs, garlic powder, salt and lemon zest in shallow dish.
Place panko crumbs in second shallow dish. Dip both sides of
turkey in egg mixture then crumb mixture. Air dry cutlets 20
minutes.

SAUTÉ turkey in butter and oil, 3 minutes on each side. Transfer
pan to oven. Roast turkey in oven for 10 minutes or until cooked
through.

Sage Pepper Sauce

- 3 tablespoons shallots, minced
- ½ cup dry, white wine
- ½ cup heavy cream
- ½ cup chicken stock
- 1 tablespoon Meyer lemon juice
- 4 tablespoons unsalted butter
- 2 teaspoons sage, minced
- ⅛ teaspoon cayenne
- ⅛ teaspoon white pepper, ground

SAUTÉ shallots 3 minutes. Add wine, cream, stock and lemon juice and reduce by half, about 10 minutes. Whisk butter in one tablespoon at a time. Finish sauce by adding sage, cayenne and white pepper. Spoon sauce on turkey. Serve immediately.

Wine: Chenin Blanc (Chappellet) or Gruet Champagne

Autumn Chicken

3 Granny Smith apples
½ lemon
4 tablespoons unsalted butter
1 tablespoon raw sugar
4 boneless chicken breasts (*fillets removed*)
1 large yellow onion, sliced
¼ cup apple cider vinegar
½ cup chicken stock

PEEL, core, and slice apples into ½-inch slices.

MELT 2 tablespoons butter in skillet, add apples, squeeze ½ lemon over apples. Sauté 5 minutes. Sprinkle with sugar. Raise to high heat, cook until browned. Set apples aside.

FLATTEN breasts with smooth meat pounder.

MELT remaining butter. Heat to medium high, add chicken and cook 3 minutes on each side. Remove.

ADD onion and cook until tender and caramelized, about 10 minutes. Raise heat to high, add vinegar and cook about one minute, down to a syrup. Add stock and stir.

RETURN chicken to pan and cook 5 minutes. Place chicken on a heated platter. Return apples to skillet to rewarm, then spoon onto chicken with juices. Serve immediately. *Serves 4*

Wine: Coastal Meadow Chardonnay (Bar Harbor Cellars, Maine)

Chicken Divan

*My friend Big Bill (6' 7") and I would periodically have cook-offs -
one month at his house with our friends, and the next month at
my house. During the cook-offs I got hooked on dill.*

2	cups broccoli, chopped
6	cups shredded chicken, cooked
2	cups button mushrooms, chopped
1	cup mayonnaise
1	cup sour cream
1	cup grated sharp cheddar cheese
½	cup whole milk
1	tablespoon fresh lemon juice
1	tablespoon fresh dill, chopped
	(or 1 teaspoon dried dill)
	salt and pepper
½	cup dry white wine
¾	cup freshly grated Gruyere *(or Swiss cheese)*
½	cup soft bread crumbs
3	tablespoons butter, melted

PREHEAT oven to 350°F. Spray an 11"x 7" casserole dish with
canola oil cooking spray.

STEAM broccoli for 4 minutes and put into casserole. Layer the
shredded chicken.

IN A MEDIUM BOWL, combine the mushrooms, mayonnaise,
sour cream, cheddar, milk, lemon juice, dill, salt and pepper to
taste, and wine and whisk. Pour the sauce over the broccoli and
chicken.

COMBINE the gruyere, bread crumbs and butter and sprinkle over
the top.

BAKE between 30 and 45 minutes.

Chicken Tortilla Soup for the Soulmate

This is one soup I make every winter to keep in the larder. It is hearty, has enough spice for extra inner body warmth and has layers of flavors that keep those taste buds in heaven.

3 tablespoons garlic infused olive oil
3 medium onions, chopped
6 garlic cloves, minced
¼ teaspoon celery seed, toasted and ground
8 cups chicken or vegetable stock
2 cups Picante *(recipe below)*
32 ounces tomatoes, chopped
2 limes, juiced
4 cups cooked chicken, chopped
6 tablespoons Worcestershire sauce
6 ounces tomato paste
6 tortilla chips
1 avocado, chopped
3 tablespoons cilantro, freshly chopped
½ cup shredded cheddar cheese
 sour cream for garnish

Picante

PUREE in food processor 2 large tomatoes, 2 jalapenos *(seeded)*, 1 large onion, 2 teaspoons apple cider vinegar, and 1 garlic clove, minced.

Soup

SAUTÉ onion and garlic in oil until tender. Add celery seed, stock, Picante, tomatoes, lime juice, chicken, Worcestershire sauce and tomato paste. Simmer 30 minutes.

PUT CHIPS in soup bowl. Add chopped avocado, cilantro, and cheese at bottom of the bowl. Ladle soup and top with sour cream.

Garlic-Rosemary Chicken

If you love garlic, this is your dish.
If you don't, beware your neighbor's breath!

2 large heads garlic
⅓ cup dry vermouth
½ cup fresh chopped rosemary
2 large chicken breasts, bone in
  salt and pepper
  rosemary sprigs for garnish

PREHEAT oven to 300°F.

CUT ½ inch of papery portion from garlic head to expose cloves, keeping cloves intact. Place garlic in small baking dish. Pour vermouth over and season with salt and pepper. Cover and bake until garlic is soft, about 1 ½ hours. Remove garlic cloves from head and squeeze garlic out of each clove into small bowl. Add chopped rosemary and mash to form smooth paste, and season with salt and pepper.

CUT chicken down backbone to butterfly. Flatten slightly. Using fingertips, loosen skin over breast. Place garlic mixture under skin, evenly covering breast. Season chicken skin with salt and pepper. Place on foil-lined baking sheet skin side up. Bake until browned and cooked through, about 55 minutes. Let stand 10 minutes.

GARNISH with fresh rosemary sprigs and serve. *Serves 4*

Wine: Chardonnay

Gingered Turkey Noodle Soup

Between the heat of the pepper and the bite of the ginger,
this soup's flavors continually layer in your mouth.

2 quarts turkey stock
1 2-inch piece of ginger, peeled and sliced ¼ inch thick
1 dried red chili
  salt and freshly ground pepper
6 medium dried shiitake mushrooms
2 cups boiling water
¾ pound spinach, large stems discarded
2 carrots, shredded
4 cups diced cooked turkey meat
  Malabar or black pepper
8 ounces rice noodles, cooked
⅓ cup thinly sliced scallions

IN A LARGE SAUCEPAN, bring the stock to a boil. Using the side of a heavy knife, smash the ginger and chili and add them to the stock. Cover and simmer for 30 minutes. Discard the ginger and chili and season the soup lightly with salt and pepper. Cover and keep hot.

IN SEPARATE heatproof bowl, cover the shiitake mushrooms with the boiling water and set aside until softened, about 10 minutes. Drain the shiitakes; cut off and discard the stems and cut the caps into thin slices.

BLANCH the spinach for 15 seconds in a medium saucepan of boiling water. Using a slotted spoon, transfer it to a colander to cool. Squeeze the spinach dry and coarsely chop it. Add the carrot to the boiling water; cook for 15 seconds. Add the carrot to the colander. Divide the noodles into 4 bowls, add turkey and season with salt and Malabar pepper. Add the shiitakes, spinach, carrot and scallions to the bowl, pour the hot stock on top and serve. *Serves 4*

Wine: Alsace Gewürztraminer or Pinot Blanc

Grilled Chicken Marsala

1	teaspoon ground fennel seeds, grind 5 seconds
1	teaspoon salt
¼	teaspoon freshly ground black pepper
⅛	teaspoon red pepper flakes
4	boneless, skinless chicken breasts *(about 6 ounces each)*
16	small carrots, peeled
1 ½	cups Marsala wine
½	cup dried Portobello mushrooms
½	cup mushroom stock
2	shallots, thinly sliced
4	cloves garlic, smashed but whole
	vegetable-oil cooking spray

HEAT up grill.

MIX fennel, salt, pepper, and red pepper flakes in a bowl. Sprinkle spice mix on both sides of chicken; set aside.

BOIL carrots for about 4 minutes, drain on a paper towel. Set aside.

BRING Marsala and mushroom stock to a low boil in a small pan over medium heat. Add mushrooms, shallots, and garlic. Season with salt and pepper. Simmer until sauce reduces, about 20 minutes. Discard garlic and set sauce aside.

COAT grill with cooking spray and grill chicken 4 to 6 minutes on each side or until cooked through. Just before you turn chicken over begin to grill carrots, about 5 minutes, rotating until charred. Return sauce to stove to warm for plate. Divide carrots among 4 plates and top with chicken, and sauce. *Serves 4*

CRITTER SUBSTITUTIONS: Wild turkey, goat and pork.

Wine: Pinot Noir

Grilled Beer Can Chicken

Debbie was making a version of this recipe using Budweiser. I said, "Sounds great, can I pick up the beer?" As a joke, I picked up a Foster's (which would only fit in a turkey!). John and Don drank the Foster's and the chicken had a Thunder Hole.

1   4-pound whole chicken
2   tablespoons canola oil
2   tablespoons sea salt
3   tablespoons grilled chicken rub *(recipe at right)*
8   ounces Bar Harbor Thunder Hole Ale *(in a can)*

134

LIGHT GRILL on medium-high on one side to warm up. Half fill a 12-ounce can with Thunder Hole Ale.

RINSE chicken inside and out, and pat dry with paper towels. Rub chicken lightly with oil then rub inside and out with salt, pepper and dry rub. Set aside.

PLACE half full can of ale on a solid surface. Grabbing a chicken leg in each hand, place the bird cavity over the beer can. Transfer the bird-on-a-can to your grill and place on the side of grill that is off, balancing the bird on its 2 legs and the can like a tripod.

COOK the chicken with the grill cover closed, for approximately 1 ¼ hours, or until the thigh juice runs clear when stabbed with a sharp knife. Remove from grill and let rest for 10 minutes before carving.

Drink: Summer Ale

My favorite dry rub for this grilled chicken:

- 4 tablespoons sweet Hungarian paprika
- 2 tablespoons chili powder
- 2 tablespoons ground, roasted cumin seeds
- 2 tablespoons dark brown sugar
- 2 tablespoons sea salt
- 1 tablespoon dried oregano
- 1 tablespoon granulated sugar
- 1 tablespoon ground black pepper
  (Lampong* peppercorns are spicy & yummy)
- 2 teaspoons cayenne pepper
- 1 teaspoon ground white pepper

MIX all ingredients together in a small bowl *(store remainder in glass container)*.

*Lampong peppercorns are available from The Spice House.

Southwest Harbor Turkey Chili

After a day of cross-country skiing or snowshoeing in Southwest Harbor, a hearty meal is on the top of our list!

2 pounds ground turkey
1 tablespoon vegetable oil
1 tablespoon butter
3 medium jalapeño peppers, stemmed, seeded and chopped
5 Poblano chili peppers, stemmed, seeded and chopped
2 yellow onions, chopped
6 garlic gloves, chopped
1 tablespoon ground cumin
2 teaspoons ground coriander
2 15-ounce cans cannellini beans, drained and rinsed
3 cups chicken broth
1 tablespoon lime juice
½ cup cilantro leaves, chopped
5 scallions, white and green parts sliced thin
salt and pepper

HEAT oil in stockpot on medium-high heat. Add ground turkey and stir to separate the meat. Cook until browned. Remove and save liquid in pot.

IN A FOOD PROCESSOR pulse the Poblanos, jalapeños and onions just until chunky. Add to stockpot and sauté. Add garlic, cumin and coriander. Cover and sauté for 10 minutes, on medium.

IN A FOOD PROCESSOR pulse 1 cup of beans and 1 cup of broth until smooth. Put mixture in stockpot with vegetables and add remaining beans, stock and ground turkey. Bring to boil then reduce to medium. Simmer, covered, stirring occasionally, for 30 minutes. Stir in remaining ingredients - lime juice, cilantro, and scallions - and stir. Add salt and pepper to taste and serve.

Mustard-Thyme Chicken Breast

½ cup chicken broth
1 small yellow onion, finely chopped
¼ cup Dijon style mustard
4 garlic cloves, finely chopped
1 teaspoon dried thyme, crumbled
¼ cup white wine *(Chardonnay)*
6 boneless skinless chicken breast halves, well trimmed
½ teaspoon ground black pepper

COMBINE first 5 ingredients in heavy large skillet. Bring to gentle simmer over medium-low heat. Add wine and chicken and season with pepper. Cover and poach until chicken is just cooked through, about 20 minutes, turning once after 10 minutes. Transfer chicken to platter. Boil liquid in skillet until reduced to sauce consistency, about 2 minutes. Pour sauce over chicken and serve. *Serves 6*

COOK'S NOTE: If you like a thicker sauce, add a mixture of 1 tablespoon flour and 1 tablespoon melted butter to sauce before reducing.

Wine: Chablis or Chardonnay

Wild Pan-Asian Turkey Loaf

Tired of the same old meatloaf? Put a little jazz in your menu!

1	tablespoon dark sesame oil
3	tablespoons chives, finely chopped
3	tablespoons carrots, finely chopped
1	teaspoon minced ginger or ½ teaspoon ginger powder
4	minced garlic cloves
1	cup precooked jasmine rice *(or white)*
¼	cup water chestnuts, chopped
3	tablespoons soy sauce
3	tablespoons Asian hot and spicy sauce*
1	pound ground wild turkey
2	tablespoons sesame seeds, toasted

PREHEAT oven to 350°F. Spray 8" x 4" loaf pan with vegetable cooking spray.

HEAT oil in non-stick skillet over medium-high heat; add chives, carrots, ginger and garlic. Sauté 4-5 minutes. Combine chive mixture in a bowl with turkey, rice, water chestnuts, soy and hot sauce. Pack into loaf pan. Top with toasted sesame seeds.

BAKE for 40-50 minutes. *Serves 6*

COOK'S NOTE: The rice is best if cooked in chicken stock. If you like less spice, start slow on the Asian hot sauce (Sambol).

*Can be purchased in international section of most grocery stores.

Partridge with Apple Cider Glaze

Cider made from fresh apples creates a full-bodied glaze for these tender breasts.

4 partridge breasts flattened to 1 inch thick
1 tablespoon vegetable oil
1 tablespoon unsalted butter
1 large onion, halved lengthwise,
   then thinly sliced crosswise
1 teaspoon sugar
¼ teaspoon salt
2 cups unfiltered apple cider
2 tablespoons apple cider vinegar

PREHEAT oven to 350°F and put oven rack in middle position.

PAT partridge breasts dry. Heat oil in cast iron skillet over moderately high heat until hot but not smoking, then brown partridge, 8 minutes per side. Transfer breasts to warm plate.

MELT butter in skillet over moderate heat until foam subsides, then cook onion with sugar and salt, scraping up brown bits and stirring occasionally with a wooden spoon, until onion is softened, 8 to 10 minutes. Add cider and vinegar and boil mixture, stirring occasionally, until onions are tender and liquid is reduced by half, about 10 minutes. Serve glaze over partridge. *Serves 4*

SUBSTITUTE CRITTERS: Chicken, pheasant, or grouse.

Wine: Chardonnay, Champagne (Korbel Brut, Gruet)

Pheasant with Shiitake Mushrooms

8	pheasant breasts (*4 whole divided in half*)
	salt and pepper
1	tablespoon porcini olive oil (*or canola oil*)
1	tablespoon unsalted butter
¾	cup shiitake mushrooms, sliced
2	leeks, white and light green parts only
½	cup white wine (*Chardonnay*)
¾	cup chicken broth
1 ½	tablespoons fresh tarragon, minced
1	cup crumbled goat cheese

PREHEAT oven to 400°F and adjust rack to middle position.

PAT pheasant dry and season with salt and pepper. Heat oil in cast iron skillet until shimmering. Cook pheasant 5 minutes on each side. Transfer pheasant to baking dish and place in oven while making sauce (no more than 6 minutes).

DISCARD remaining oil in skillet. Melt butter in empty skillet over high until foaming. Add mushrooms and leeks and cook until liquid evaporates, about 4 minutes. Add wine and cook about 1 minute. Add broth and 1 tablespoon tarragon and simmer until thickened, about 5 minutes. Whisk in goat cheese and simmer another minute. Add remaining tarragon and season with salt and pepper.

RETURN pheasant to skillet and coat with sauce. Serve immediately.

Wine: Chardonnay

Rosemary Citrus Chicken

This chicken dish paired with the
Jasmine-Ginger Rice (recipe p. 22) is a crowd pleaser.

6	large boneless chicken breasts
½	cup chicken broth
½	cup crushed pineapple
	juice from one small orange
	zest from one small orange
½	cup brown sugar
2	tablespoons Dijon style mustard
¼	cup balsamic vinegar
1	tablespoon garlic, minced
1	tablespoon ginger, grated
2	teaspoons fresh rosemary, chopped
1	teaspoon salt
1	cup onions, minced

PREHEAT oven to 350°F.

MIX all ingredients together, except chicken and onions. Place chicken in marinade and refrigerate for 3 hours before baking, turning once. Place chicken in a greased roasting pan and top with onions. Pour enough marinade back over chicken to coat onions and bottom of the pan. Cover with aluminum foil and bake for 30 minutes. Remove cover and bake another 10 minutes.

COOK'S NOTE: This is a great marinade for grilled chicken.

Wine: David Bruce Pinot Noir, Columbia Crest Chardonnay

Seared Chicken and Sun-Dried Tomatoes on Angel Hair

1   pound angel hair pasta
1   tablespoon corn starch
¼   cup skim milk
¼   cup balsamic vinegar
1   teaspoon salt
½   cup water
1   tablespoon porcini olive oil
3   boneless chicken breasts, halved
2   cloves garlic, thinly sliced
¼   cup sun-dried tomatoes, soaked in hot water for 10 minutes, drained
½   pound asparagus, cut in ½-inch diagonal pieces
½   pound shiitake mushrooms, sliced
¼   cup grated Parmesan (or Asiago)

COOK pasta 2 minutes less than the package indicates. Drain, set aside. Mix corn starch, milk, vinegar, salt and ½ cup water in a bowl, set aside.

HEAT porcini olive oil in skillet to high heat. Sear chicken, 3 minutes on each side. Lower to medium heat. Add garlic, tomatoes, asparagus and mushrooms. Cook 3 more minutes, or until chicken is no longer pink in center and vegetables begin to soften. Reduce heat to low and stir in cooked pasta and corn starch mixture. Cook 2 or 3 minutes until sauce begins to thicken. Sprinkle with cheese and serve immediately. *Serves 4*

Smoked Duck in Raspberry Sauce

Marinade

2   ¾-pound duck breasts
    salt and freshly ground pepper
1   cup Cabernet Sauvignon
2   tablespoons raspberry vinegar

PAT duck dry. Salt and pepper both sides. Combine wine and vinegar in a shallow bowl. Marinate duck for 6 hours in refrigerator before smoking. Smoke in electric smoker on 225°F for 45 minutes for a medium center.

Sauce

2   tablespoons unsalted butter
1   shallot, minced
¼   cup dry white wine
½   cup ruby port
2   tablespoons seedless raspberry preserves
1   tablespoon raspberry vinegar
1   tablespoon Dijon style mustard
½   cup raspberries
    salt and freshly ground pepper

MELT 1 tablespoon of the butter in a medium saucepan. Add the shallot and cook over moderate heat, stirring frequently, until softened, about 2 minutes. Add the white wine and port and cook over moderate heat until the sauce is reduced to 2 tablespoons, about 7 minutes. Add the raspberry preserves, vinegar and mustard and whisk over low heat until smooth. Add the raspberries and cook, whisking gently to break up the berries. Whisk in the remaining 1 tablespoon of butter and season with salt and pepper; keep the sauce warm.

REMOVE duck from smoker, let rest 5 minutes. Slice on the diagonal and serve on warm plate with sauce.

Smoked Wild Goose

*Thanks to Ron and Mike Musetti I get an annual
supply of geese to test recipes.*

2 ½ cups water
1 ½ cups soy sauce
1 ½ cups pineapple juice
   1 cup dry sherry
   1 cup sugar
   ½ cup salt
   1 tablespoon onion powder
   8 garlic cloves, minced
   4 tablespoons minced fresh ginger

COMBINE all ingredients to make marinade. Soak goose
overnight.

PUMP marinade out. Pat goose dry and air dry for four hours.

PLACE bird on greased racks in electric smokehouse for 3-4 hours
on 225°F. Use 2 pans of chips *(add new bunch after 1 ½ hours)*.

Wine: Petite Syrah

Tarragon and Tomato Partridge

4 tablespoons olive oil
2 tablespoons unsalted butter
2 partridge breasts, cut into serving pieces
  salt and pepper
2 onions, cut into large chunks
5 garlic cloves, chopped
4 carrots, chopped *(2 yellow and 2 orange)*
1 cup tarragon vinegar
2 pounds ripe tomatoes, seeded and chopped
2 cups dry white wine *(Pouilly-Fuisse)*
2 tablespoons dried tarragon
1 teaspoon dried thyme
¼ cup chicken stock
½ teaspoon ground Lampong black pepper
¼ cup tomato paste

HEAT oil and butter in large, deep skillet. Salt and pepper the partridge and brown for 3 to 4 minutes on each side. Remove the partridge from the pan and set aside.

SAUTÉ onions until tender. Add the remaining ingredients, except tomato paste. Bring the liquid up to a simmer and cook for 15 minutes. Stir tomato paste into vegetable mixture. Add the partridge back to the pan and continue to simmer for 20 minutes. Serve on top of noodles lightly tossed with butter or olive oil. *Serves 2*

Marinated Wild Turkey Breast

4 turkey breasts, pressed to ¾ inch thickness
1 cup water
1 cup onions, minced
¾ cup corn syrup
½ cup crushed pineapple
½ cup orange juice
½ cup brown sugar
2 tablespoons whole cranberry honey mustard
¼ cup balsamic vinegar
1 tablespoon roasted garlic
1 teaspoon dried garlic
1 tablespoon powdered ginger
2 teaspoons rosemary
1 teaspoon salt

MIX all ingredients except turkey. Marinate turkey breasts 2 hours. Grill on medium heat, turning once after 7 minutes. Baste with remaining marinade after turning.

SUBSTITUTE CRITTERS: Chicken, wild boar or pork loin.

Wine: Pinot Noir (Castlerock)

Smoked Turkey Soup

*You wouldn't believe the difference this pepper makes in the soup.
It provides the gentlest after-heat that begs for more in your bowl.
The rich, homemade stock heals the sick.*

8   cups Smoked Turkey Stock *(see recipe p. 188, or chicken broth)*
2   cups yellow onion, chopped
6   carrots, chopped
1   medium sweet potato, skinned and chopped
3   Maine potatoes, skinned and chopped
4   cups smoked turkey meat, diced
1   teaspoon salt
1   tablespoon Tortollan herbed pepper* *(or black pepper)*

IN A LARGE SAUCEPAN, bring the stock to a boil. Add the onions, carrots and sweet potato and cook for 10 minutes, add Maine potatoes, turkey meat and pepper and simmer for 30 minutes.

Tortollan herbed pepper is available from Sunny Caribbee Spice Co. Ltd., see Resources.

Desserts

Maine Maple Brown Betty
Almond Biscotti
Apple Pie with Graham Flour Crust
Chocolate Toffee Cookies
Baby Boomer Whoopie Pies
Banana Bread
Buttermilk Pound Cake
Goat's Milk Peanut Butter Fudge
Carrot Cake with Cream Cheese Frosting
Chocolate Zucchini Muffins
French Crunch Peach Pie with Roasted Walnut Pie Crust
Triple Chunky Ginger Cookies
Gingerbread Scones
Jackman Gingerbread
Kirstie's Christmas Sugar Cookies
Lemon Black Fly Muffins
Maine Blueberry Pie
Maple Apple Pie
Northern Comfort Balls
Moose Balls
Pecan Snow Balls
Simple Truffles
Orange Zest Cake
Pumpkin Roll
Roasted Walnut Drops
Strawberry Pie with Chestnut Flour Crust
Very Ginger Cake
White Chocolate Macadamia Drops
Wicked Gingerbread Cake

149

Maine Maple Brown Betty

*I went round and round with some of my testers on the original
too-long name. Typically, you try and capture some
key ingredients; in this dish they are all key.*

½	cup butter, room temperature
¾	cup rolled oats
¼	cup flour
¼	cup graham flour
¾	cup dark brown sugar *(packed)*
1	teaspoon nutmeg
1	teaspoon cinnamon
¼	teaspoon mace
⅛	teaspoon allspice ground
⅓	cup water
½	cup Roasted Maple-Gingered Pecans *(recipe p. 25)*, chopped
3	tablespoons Maine maple syrup
4	cups apples, peeled and sliced *(I use Northern Spy or Granny Smith)*

PREHEAT oven to 375°F.

COMBINE the brown sugar, oats, flours, cinnamon, nutmeg, mace, pecans and butter and stir with a fork until well-mixed and crumbly.

LAYER one third of the apples, then one third of the crumb mixture in a greased, 7" x 11" baking dish. Repeat until all apples and crumb mixture are added.

POUR water over the mixture and bake for 30 minutes. Serve warm with Maine's Gifford French Vanilla ice cream.

Almond Biscotti

If you really want to indulge, either spread a little Nutella® or melt chocolate to dip these in!

½ cup sugar
2 tablespoons butter, room temperature
1 large egg
1 teaspoon almond extract
⅛ teaspoon ground star of anise
1 cup flour
¼ cup almond flour
¼ cup sliced almonds
1 teaspoon baking powder
½ teaspoon nutmeg, freshly ground
⅛ teaspoon salt

PREHEAT oven to 350°F.

COMBINE sugar and butter until blended. Combine flour, baking powder, nutmeg and salt gradually into sugar mixture.

TURN dough onto floured surface and knead 7 times. Roll out to 1 inch thickness, 12 inches long and 7 or 8 inches wide. Place roll on cookie sheet. Bake for 30 minutes. Cool on wire rack for 5 minutes. Slice diagonally in ¾ inch slices. Place cookies on their sides on baking sheet and bake 5 minutes more. Turn cookies over and bake 5 more minutes on second side. Cool completely on wire rack. Biscotti will harden as they cool. *Yields 12-15 biscotti.*

COOK'S NOTE: Can substitute 1 teaspoon almond extract and ⅛ teaspoon anise for 1 teaspoon powdered ginger and 1 teaspoon minced candied ginger.

Apple Pie with Graham Flour Crust

We pick apples right out our front door. I use Northern Spy for this recipe, however, Granny Smiths are perfect too.

6	cups Granny Smith apples, peeled and sliced
1	cup sugar
1	teaspoon Vietnamese Cassia "Saigon" Cinnamon, ground fine (*The Spice House, see Resources*)
¼	teaspoon nutmeg, ground fine
⅛	teaspoon mace, ground fine
2	tablespoons tapioca

COMBINE sugar, spices and tapioca. Add mixture to apples and toss to coat. Fill pastry shell with apple mixture and cover with top crust. Cover edges of pie with foil.

BAKE in 375°F oven for 20 minutes. Remove foil. Bake 25 - 30 more minutes or until golden crust. Cool on wire rack.
Makes 8 servings.

Pie Crust

3 ⅓	cups white flour
⅔	cup graham flour
1	tablespoon vanilla sugar
¼	teaspoon salt
1 ¾	cups vegetable shortening
½	cup cold water
1	tablespoon apple cider vinegar
1	large egg

CUT vegetable shortening into flours. Beat egg and vinegar into cold water. Mix into flour and shortening and roll out.

Makes 1 double pie crust

Chocolate Toffee Cookies

        8   tablespoons butter, room temperature
        ¾   cup dark brown sugar
        ¼   cup granulated vanilla sugar*
        1   large egg
    1 ½   cups flour
        ½   teaspoon baking soda
        ¼   teaspoon salt
        1   teaspoon vanilla extract
        1   cup toffee chips *(or chopped up Skor bar)*
        ½   cup chocolate semi-sweet chips
              nutmeg, grated *(a whisper)*

PREHEAT oven to 350°F.

CREAM butter and sugars then add egg and vanilla. Add dry ingredients, mix. Fold in toffee and chocolate chips. Drop by tablespoon onto un-greased cookie sheet.

BAKE for 10 minutes.

*COOK'S NOTE: Vanilla sugar - cut vanilla bean open and scrape out seeds. Place seeds in glass jar with 3 cups of sugar. Let stand for 2 weeks in cupboard before use. Store out of the sun in dark cabinet.

Baby Boomer Whoopie Pies

Growing up we looked forward to these yummy cakes and my mom's infamous hard frosting in the middle. The recipe has been changed to accommodate our generation.

½ cup shortening
1 cup sugar
2 egg yolks, beaten until light-colored
1 teaspoon vanilla
1 tablespoon espresso powder
2 teaspoons hot water
6 tablespoons sweet cocoa powder
2 cups sifted flour
1 teaspoon baking powder
1 teaspoon baking soda
½ teaspoon salt
1 cup whole milk

PREHEAT oven to 375°F.

CREAM together shortening and sugar. Add beaten egg yolks, then vanilla. Dissolve espresso in hot water and whip this into wet mixture. Sift all dry ingredients together and add half to creamed mixture, stir, then add second half. Add milk and mix well.

DROP by tablespoons onto ungreased non-stick cookie sheet. Bake for 8 to 10 minutes depending upon the size you make. Cool. Put together with the following filling and wrap each separately with wax paper.

Filling

  - ¾ cup shortening
  - 1 teaspoon almond extract
  - 2 cups powdered sugar
  - ¼ cup whole milk, room temperature

CREAM shortening and extract. Fold in half the powdered sugar and half the milk, then the remaining powdered sugar.

ADD remaining milk for softer filling.

COOK'S NOTE: You can substitute water for milk in the filling. These freeze well either way.

Banana Bread

This is great right out of the oven with peanut butter and ice cream.

  - 1 stick butter
  - ½ cup brown sugar
  - ½ cup white sugar
  - 2 eggs
  - 3 medium, very ripe bananas
  - ½ cup buttermilk
  - 2 cups white flour
  - ⅓ cup graham flour
  - 1 ¼ teaspoons baking soda
  - 1 teaspoon baking powder
  - ½ teaspoon salt
  - 1 cup chopped walnuts

PREHEAT oven to 350°F. Grease 9" x 5" loaf pan.

CREAM sugars and butter in large mixing bowl. Add one egg at a time and beat until fluffy. Add bananas and buttermilk and mix. In a separate bowl combine remaining dry ingredients. Add to mixture and blend. Fold in walnuts.

POUR into loaf pan. Bake for 55 minutes or until toothpick comes out clean when inserted in center. Cool on wire rack.

Buttermilk Pound Cake

2 ¼   cups white flour
¾   cup graham flour (*or wheat*)
1 ½   teaspoons baking powder
¼   teaspoon salt
3   large eggs
½   cup fresh buttermilk
½   cup canola oil
2   tablespoons light corn syrup
1   tablespoon vanilla extract
6   large egg whites
2   cups sugar, divided
1   stick unsalted butter
8   ounces low fat cream cheese
your favorite preserves*

PREHEAT oven to 325°F. Coat bundt pan with cooking spray and dust with flour, do not use spray with flour.

WHISK flours, baking powder, and salt in medium bowl. In another medium bowl whisk 3 eggs, buttermilk, oil, corn syrup and vanilla.

BEAT egg whites in large clean bowl with electric mixer on high speed until light and foamy. Gradually beat in ¼ cup sugar until stiff glossy peaks.

BEAT butter and cream cheese in a large bowl until creamy. Add remaining 1 ¾ cups sugar and beat, scraping down the sides of bowl as needed until pale and fluffy, about 4 minutes. Alternately add flour then buttermilk mixtures, beating until smooth. Fold in one third of the egg whites with a rubber spatula until just smooth and no white streaks remain. Fold in the remaining egg whites. Scrape batter into pan and spreading evenly.

BAKE 1 hour and 10 minutes. Cool in pan on wire rack for 10 minutes. Loosen edge with knife and turn onto rack and cool 1 hour more before slicing.

*COOK'S NOTE: Bonus - heat ½ cup of your favorite preserves with 1 tablespoon water *(for a shiny glaze put the heated preserves through a sieve before brushing on the cake)*, drizzle over the cake.

Goat's Milk Peanut Butter Fudge

This is the absolute BEST fudge I have ever had or made. I was at the Cumberland Fair back in 1980 with my girlfriend, Devorah Rifka, and we tried their goat's milk peanut fudge. It is so creamy because goat's milk does not separate like cow's milk and is a much richer fudge without that sugary grit. I took an old recipe of my Nana's (Penelope Hall), made a couple changes and voilà!

- 2 cups granulated sugar
- 2 cups dark brown sugar
- ¾ cup goat's milk
- ½ teaspoon salt
- 18 ounces creamy peanut butter
- 8 ounces marshmallow fluff
- 1 tablespoon vanilla

COMBINE over high heat granulated sugar, brown sugar, goat's milk and salt to firm-ball stage (250°F), about 5 minutes. Remove from heat and add the remaining ingredients, stirring constantly until combined. Pour into 8" x 13" pan. Chill, cut and serve.

Carrot Cake with Cream Cheese Frosting

Fresh carrots from the garden make this cake's flavor over the top.

1 ½ cups canola oil
2 cups sugar
4 large eggs
¼ cup pineapple juice
3 cups fresh carrots, grated
2 cups flour
2 teaspoons cinnamon
2 teaspoons baking soda
1 teaspoon nutmeg
1 teaspoon salt

PREHEAT oven to 350°F.

CREAM sugar and oil in large mixing bowl. Add one egg at a time and beat until fluffy. Add juice and carrots and mix. In a separate bowl combine remaining dry ingredients. Fold into wet mixture and blend.

SPRAY non-stick spray and then flour two 8" round cake pans and divide batter equally. Bake 45 minutes or until toothpick is inserted in center and pulled out dry. Cool on wire rack and frost.

Cream Cheese Frosting

8 ounces cream cheese, room temperature
1 stick butter, room temperature
1 pound powdered sugar
½ teaspoon vanilla extract

BEAT cream cheese and butter until fluffy. Add vanilla and gradually beat in powdered sugar. Chill 30 minutes before frosting cake.

Chocolate Zucchini Muffins

*I have tried so many versions of this recipe and
I like the moistness in this one.*

1	stick butter
½	cup canola oil
1 ¼	cups white sugar
¼	cup brown sugar
2	large eggs
1	teaspoon vanilla
2	cups grated zucchini
2	cups flour
1	teaspoon soda
5	tablespoons unsweetened cocoa
1	teaspoon cinnamon
½	teaspoon nutmeg
¼	teaspoon salt
½	cup chocolate bits
½	cup walnuts

PREHEAT oven to 325°F.

CREAM butter, canola oil and sugars. Add eggs and beat. Add
vanilla, zucchini and mix. Whip in flour, baking soda, cocoa, spices
and salt. Fold in chocolate bits and nuts.

SPRAY regular sized muffin tins with non-stick spray. Spoon into
muffin cups and bake for 30 minutes. Cool on wire rack.

French Crunch Peach Pie with Roasted Walnut Pie Crust

When you have a tester that doesn't like peaches and enjoys the recipe, you know you did something right!

2   large eggs
1   tablespoon lemon juice
¼   cup brown sugar
¼   cup white sugar
6   cups fresh, sliced peaches *(or 48 ounces canned peaches, drained and patted dry)*
1   cup vanilla wafers, finely crushed
½   cup walnuts, roasted and chopped *(see below)*
¼   cup salted butter, melted

PREHEAT oven to 450°F.

ROAST whole walnuts in dry cast iron skillet for 5 minutes, stirring constantly. Cool before chopping.

BAKE pie crust *(recipe at right)* for 5 minutes, then lower oven to 375°F. Beat eggs and lemon juice until combined; stir in sugars. Fold in peaches. Turn peach mixture in partially baked pie crust. Stir together vanilla wafer crumbs, walnuts and butter. Sprinkle over peach mixture. Cover edges of pie with foil.

BAKE in 375°F oven for 20 minutes. Remove foil. Bake 25 - 30 more minutes or until crust is golden. Cool on wire rack. *Serves 8*

Pie Crust

¼   cup roasted walnut oil *(or canola oil)*
¼   cup canola oil
6   tablespoons cold milk
2 ¼   cups white flour
½   teaspoon salt

POUR oil and milk into measuring cup *(do not stir)*. Add to flour and salt in mixing bowl. Stir with fork. Form 2 balls and flatten them slightly with hands.

PLACE each ball between 2 sheets of wax paper and roll into circle. Dampen work surface to keep wax paper from slipping. Peel off top paper and place in pie plate. Take off top paper and fill.

161

Makes 1 double pie crust (this crust is great for pumpkin pie too).

Triple Chunky Ginger Cookies

2 cups flour
2 ½ teaspoons ground ginger
2 teaspoons baking soda
1 teaspoon ground cinnamon
1 teaspoon ground cloves
¼ teaspoon salt
¾ cup crystallized ginger cut in ¼ inch chunks
1 cup light brown sugar
½ cup unsalted butter
¼ cup canola oil
1 egg
¼ cup dark molasses
1 teaspoon fresh ginger juice *
sugar to coat

162

PREHEAT oven at 350° F.

MIX the first six dry ingredients in a medium bowl. Whisk together and add the ginger chunks. Separately, cream the butter, oil and brown sugar; add the egg, molasses and fresh ginger juice. Mix well. Fold in the dry flour mixture. Cover and chill for 1 hour.

BUTTER baking sheets. Form balls with the dough, using the palms of your hands. Roll the cookie dough balls in ginger sugar (toss fresh cut up ginger from ginger juice into white sugar in Ziploc bag), or use regular white sugar.

BAKE for 10-12 minutes. Cool on wire racks.

*COOK'S NOTE: A garlic press works great to juice fresh ginger. Cut the pieces *(lengthwise so as not to get stuck in garlic press)* and juice ginger over a small bowl. Be careful to clean it well beforehand to prevent any garlic flavor mixing in with the ginger juice.

Gingerbread Scones

   2   cups flour
   ½   cup dark brown sugar
   1   tablespoon baking powder
   ¾   teaspoon cinnamon
   ½   teaspoon powdered ginger
   ⅛   teaspoon cloves
   6   tablespoons chilled butter
   1   teaspoon ginger juice *(see previous COOK'S NOTE)*
   ¼   cup milk
   1   large egg
   3   tablespoons molasses
   1   teaspoon vanilla extract

PREHEAT oven to 375°F.

COMBINE first 6 ingredients in processor. Add butter and pulse until mixture resembles coarse meal. Beat ginger juice, milk, egg, molasses, and vanilla to blend in large bowl. Add flour mixture and gently stir until dough forms. Roll dough into ball.

ON LIGHTLY FLOURED SURFACE, press dough into 1-inch thick round. Cut into 8 wedges. Place on non-stick baking sheet about an inch apart.

BAKE until toothpick inserted into center comes out clean, about 25 minutes. Serve warm or at room temperature

Jackman Gingerbread

I worked for Scott Paper Company in the summer of 1978. I was the first woman in the woods on the road crew in Jackman. What a memorable summer! Coworker Pat Goode gave me the base of this recipe. The boiling water makes it so moist!

½   cup butter
½   cup molasses
½   cup brown sugar, packed
1 ½   cups flour
½   teaspoon baking soda
½   teaspoon baking powder
¾   teaspoon powdered ginger
¾   teaspoon ground cinnamon
¼   teaspoon allspice
1   cup boiling water
     whip cream
     nutmeg for grated garnish

PREHEAT oven to 350°F.

CREAM butter, molasses and sugar together. Mix dry ingredients separately and fold into wet ingredients. Add boiling water and stir until mixed. Pour into greased and floured 8" x 8" pan.

BAKE for 30 minutes. Cool and serve with whip cream on top and a quick grate of fresh nutmeg.

COOK'S NOTE: The batter will be very runny when pouring it into cake pan.

Kirstie's Christmas Sugar Cookies

My niece, Kirstie, makes an annual pilgrimage to our house
before Christmas to make cookies for all her friends.
This is her favorite cookie to decorate.

1   cup butter, unsalted
1   cup white sugar
2   eggs, slightly beaten
1   teaspoon vanilla
3   cups flour
2   teaspoons baking powder
1   teaspoon salt

PREHEAT oven to 350°F.

CREAM the butter and sugar in a bowl. Beat in the eggs and vanilla. In a second bowl, combine flour, baking powder and salt. Stir flour into creamed mixture. Chill dough for 3 or 4 hours. Roll out dough to about ¼ inch and cut into shapes with cookie cutters. Bake on a non-stick cookie pan or stone cookie sheet.

BAKE for 12-15 minutes. Cool cookies on wire rack.

COOK'S NOTE: Decorate before they go in the oven - brush with milk and sprinkle with colored sugar. Or decorate after they come out of the oven - let them cool and let your creative juices flow!

Lemon Black Fly Muffins

These are my favorite muffins, and favorites for everyone else who has tried them.

½ cup canola oil
¾ cup Splenda®
1 egg
1 egg white
1 cup lemon yogurt
¼ teaspoon Meyer lemon zest *(or regular lemon)*
1 tablespoon Meyer lemon juice
1 ½ cups flour
½ teaspoon baking soda
¼ teaspoon salt
1 tablespoon black flies *(or poppy seeds)*

PREHEAT oven to 325°F.

COMBINE canola oil and Splenda®. Add eggs and mix. Add yogurt, lemon zest and juice and mix. Fold in flour, baking soda, salt and black flies *(or poppy seeds)*.

SPRAY regular sized muffin tins with non-stick cooking spray. Spoon into muffin tins and bake for 25 minutes. Cool on wire rack. Makes 12 small or 6 large muffins.

SUBSTITUTIONS: Vanilla yogurt and blueberries, or orange juice and orange zest with whole chopped cranberries, or any combination that sounds good to you. These muffins don't rise up as much as with regular sugar, but they are so moist and yummy you do not miss the sugar. You can also substitute regular sugar for the Splenda®.

Maine Blueberry Pie

  1 cup sugar
  2 tablespoons tapioca
  ½ teaspoon Meyer lemon zest
  ⅛ teaspoon salt
  5 cups fresh blueberries
  2 teaspoons Meyer lemon juice

PREHEAT oven to 350°F.

COMBINE sugar, tapioca, lemon zest and salt. Toss with blueberries until coated. Fill crust with berry mixture. Drizzle lemon juice over blueberries and top with crust and seal edges. Cover edges of pie with foil. *(If using frozen blueberries, add ¼ cup flour to berry mixture.)*

BAKE for 20 minutes. Remove foil. Bake 25 - 30 more minutes or until crust is golden. Cool on wire rack. *Makes 8 servings.*

Pie Crust

  4 cups white flour
  2 tablespoons sugar
  ¼ teaspoon salt
  1 ¾ cups vegetable shortening
  ½ cup cold water
  2 tablespoons apple cider vinegar
  1 large egg

CUT vegetable shortening into flour. Beat egg and vinegar into cold water. Mix into flour and shortening. *Makes 1 double pie crust.*

Maple Apple Pie

*My Uncle Gary makes homemade maple syrup and I am lucky
enough to get some. What a difference!*

Crust

4	cups white flour
¼	teaspoon salt
1 ¾	cups vegetable shortening
½	cup cold water
3	tablespoons apple cider vinegar
1	large egg

168

PREHEAT oven to 375°F.

CUT shortening into flour and salt, using pastry blender or fork,
until mixture resembles coarse crumbs. Beat egg and vinegar into
cold water. Mix into flour and shortening until dough is just moist
enough to form a ball when lightly pressed together. Shape dough
into 2 balls.

FLATTEN 1 ball to ½-inch thickness on lightly floured surface, roll
from center to edge into 11" circle. Fold pastry in half; place in a 9"
pie plate. Unfold; gently press in bottom and up the sides of the
pan. Do not stretch. Trim pastry even with an edge. Roll out
remaining pastry; set aside.

Filling

7	cups Northern Spy *(Granny Smith)* apples, peeled and sliced
1	cup maple syrup
2	tablespoons tapioca

1 teaspoon cinnamon
¼ teaspoon nutmeg
½ teaspoon salt

COMBINE all ingredients and mix to coat apples. Place apples into pastry lined pie plate. Top with remaining pastry. Brush top of pie with milk to aid in browning. Foil edges so they won't burn.

BAKE in 375°F oven for 20 minutes. Remove foil. Bake 25 - 30 more minutes or until golden crust. Cool on wire rack. Add a little Gifford's ice cream! *Makes 8 servings.*

Northern Comfort Balls

These will warm the cockles of your heart in the dead of winter.

1 cup vanilla wafers, finely crushed
1 cup powdered sugar
2 tablespoons cocoa
2 tablespoons light corn syrup
¼ cup Southern Comfort
1 ½ cups chopped walnuts
½ cup granulated sugar

COMBINE all ingredients, except nuts and granulated sugar. Roll in little balls, and then roll the balls in the walnuts and granulated sugar.

COOK'S NOTE: I also like rolling them in toasted coconut or finely ground dried cranberries.

Moose Balls

Thanks Anne for getting me started on a great holiday tradition! Like the espresso?

Filling

4   sticks butter, room temperature
2   pounds powdered sugar
4   teaspoons vanilla
2   cups peanut butter

MIX all ingredients, and chill. Roll into balls, place on waxed paper and freeze for 1 hour.

Chocolate

1   tablespoon espresso powder
2   tablespoons hot water
¼   cup paraffin wax
1   large bag chocolate chips

MIX espresso powder with hot water. Stir until dissolved.
In a double boiler heat chocolate chips, paraffin wax, and espresso mixture. Stir until melted. Keep heat on simmer after mixture has completed melted.

ONE at a time dip frozen moose balls into the chocolate mixture. Chill and serve.

COOK'S NOTE: can freeze for up to 3 months.

Pecan Snow Balls

Another holiday tradition in our house.

½	cup sweet butter, softened
1 ½	teaspoons vanilla
2	cups flour
1	cup pecans, finely chopped
6	tablespoons powdered sugar, for rolling

PREHEAT oven to 300°F, with a rack placed low.

MIX all ingredients together. Roll into small balls and place on ungreased jelly roll pan.

BAKE on a low rack for 30 minutes. While still warm, roll in powdered sugar. These cookies freeze well for a month in a sealed bag.

Simple Truffles

½	pound semi-sweet chocolate, chopped fine
½	pound bittersweet chocolate, chopped fine
1	cup cream, hot
1	teaspoon expresso powder
½	tablespoon hot water
1	teaspoon vanilla
	good cocoa powder

SLOWLY stir hot cream into chocolate until melted.

DISSOLVE expresso powder in hot water and add to chocolate mixture. Add vanilla and cool for 1 hour. Roll in balls, then roll balls in cocoa powder. Store or serve.

Orange Zest Cake

Thanks to many testers in the Ferm Family,
this recipe made it into the pages of this cookbook!

2 sticks unsalted butter, softened
3 cups flour
3 oranges for zest and juice
2 tablespoons freshly squeezed lemon juice
2 ⅓ cups sugar
3 large eggs
½ teaspoon baking soda
½ teaspoon salt
1 cup buttermilk *(fresh not powdered)*
1 cup powdered sugar

PREHEAT oven to 350°F.

BUTTER and flour bundt pan. Zest and juice oranges.

MIX ½ cup orange juice, 1 tablespoon lemon juice, ½ cup sugar and zest. Set aside zest mixture.

CREAM butter and sugar until fluffy. Add eggs, one at a time and mix. Add 1½ cups flour, baking soda, and salt and mix. Add half buttermilk and mix. Repeat with remaining flour and buttermilk. Add zest mixture and combine.

POUR dough into pan and place on baking sheet. Bake 1 to 1 ¼ hours. Cool in pan 15 minutes. Loosen cake with knife. Turn onto wire rack. Cool.

GLAZE: While cake is baking, mix remaining lemon and orange juice together. Whisk in powdered sugar for glaze. Using pastry brush spread glaze over top of cake while warm and let soak in.

Pumpkin Roll

The inspiration for this recipe came from a friend of a friend of a friend; many hands later, here is a Thanksgiving tradition dessert.

Roll

3 large eggs
1 cup sugar
⅔ cup fresh pumpkin
1 teaspoon lemon juice
¾ cup flour
½ teaspoon salt
1 teaspoon baking powder
1 teaspoon cinnamon
½ teaspoon nutmeg

Filling

8 ounces cream cheese, room temperature
4 tablespoons butter, room temperature
1 cup powdered sugar
1 teaspoon vanilla

PREHEAT oven to 350°F.

WHISK eggs and sugar. Add pumpkin and lemon juice and stir. Add dry ingredients and stir well. In another bowl whip cream cheese and butter, add vanilla and sugar until blended, set aside.

GREASE jelly roll pan, line with wax paper, and grease paper. Pour pumpkin mix in pan, bake 15 minutes or until golden brown. Place clean dishtowel on top and carefully roll lengthwise, and cool.

UNROLL cooled pumpkin, peel off wax paper, spread on filling, roll up and chill. Slice and serve.

Roasted Walnut Drops

This is a deadly recipe. I don't know which I like better, the dough or the cookie!

2	sticks unsalted butter, soft
2	tablespoons roasted walnut oil*
1	cup dark brown sugar
½	cup granulated sugar
2	medium eggs
2	teaspoons vanilla extract *(pure)*
¼	teaspoon salt
2 ½	cups flour
2	cups finely chopped walnuts

174

PREHEAT oven to 350°F.

CREAM butter, sugars, and walnut oil until smooth. Add eggs and mix, add vanilla and salt and mix. Gently mix in flour and walnuts.

DROP by teaspoons on ungreased cookie sheet. Bake 9-10 minutes. Cool on wire rack. *Makes 3-4 dozen cookies.*

COOK'S NOTE: Dough freezes well up to 1 month.

* Supermarkets are beginning to carry different flavored oils such as this one, or try Le Roux in Portland, Maine.

Strawberry Pie with Chestnut Flour Crust

1	cup sugar
2	tablespoons tapioca *(long cooking)*
⅛	teaspoon salt
¼	teaspoon butter rum extract
4	cups fresh strawberries, sliced

COMBINE sugar, tapioca and salt. Pour extract over strawberries, then toss with sugar mixture until coated. Fill crust with berry mixture and top with crust (see below) and seal edges.

COVER edges of pie with foil.

BAKE in 375°F oven for 20 minutes. Remove foil. Bake 25 - 30 more minutes or until crust is golden. Cool on wire rack. *Makes 8 servings.*

Pie Crust

3 ¼	cups white flour
¾	cup chestnut flour
3	tablespoons vanilla sugar
1 ¾	cups vegetable shortening
1	large egg
4	tablespoons apple cider vinegar
½	cup cold water

CUT vegetable shortening into the two flours and vanilla sugar. Beat egg and vinegar into cold water. Mix into flour and shortening. *Makes 1 double pie crust.*

Very Ginger Cake

1 ¼ cups white flour
¼ cup graham flour
1 teaspoon baking soda
¼ teaspoon salt
½ cup packed brown sugar
¼ cup molasses
¼ cup honey
1 large egg
½ cup minced fresh ginger
½ teaspoon powdered ginger
1 teaspoon granulated candied ginger
1 stick unsalted butter
½ cup water
powdered sugar

PREHEAT oven to 350°F. Spray nonstick baking spray and line bottom of 9" square baking dish with parchment or wax paper.

WHISK first four ingredients together. In second bowl cream sugar, molasses, honey and egg together. Whisk in gingers.

MELT butter in small saucepan with water. Whisk into molasses mixture then add flour and mix just until smooth.

POUR batter into baking dish. Bake for 30 minutes. Allow cake to cool in dish for 10 minutes. Slide thick knife around edge to loosen from dish. Invert cake onto a plate, and then invert again onto cooling rack, right side up, and peel off paper lining. When cool, sprinkle with powdered sugar.

White Chocolate Macadamia Drops

  1   stick butter, room temperature
  ¾   cup dark brown sugar
  ¼   cup granulated vanilla sugar*
  1   large egg
  1   teaspoon vanilla extract
1 ½   cups flour
  ½   teaspoon baking soda
  ¼   teaspoon salt
  1   cup white chocolate chips
  ½   cup unsalted macadamia nuts, chopped
       nutmeg, grated *(a whisper)*

PREHEAT oven to 350°F.

CREAM butter and sugars, then add egg and vanilla. Add flour, baking soda and salt, mix. Fold in white chocolate chips and macadamia nuts. Drop by tablespoon onto un-greased cookie sheet. Bake for 9 minutes.

*COOK'S NOTE: Vanilla sugar - cut vanilla bean open and scrape out seeds. Cut bean pod in thirds. Place seeds and bean pod in glass jar with 3 cups of granulated sugar. Let stand for 2 weeks in cupboard before use. Store out of the sun in dark cabinet.

Wicked Gingerbread Cake

1	cup Guinness® Extra Stout or other dark beer
1	cup mild flavored molasses
1 ½	teaspoons baking soda
2	cups all-purpose flour
2	tablespoons ground ginger
1 ½	teaspoons baking powder
¾	teaspoon ground cinnamon
¼	teaspoon ground cloves
¼	teaspoon fresh ground nutmeg
⅛	teaspoon ground cardamon
3	large eggs
½	cup sugar
½	cup *(packed)* dark brown sugar
¾	cup vegetable oil
1	tablespoon fresh ginger, minced
2	tablespoons candied ginger, finely chopped *(for top of cake)*

PREHEAT oven to 350°F.

BUTTER and flour three 8" cake pans. Bring stout and molasses to boil in a heavy medium-size non-reactive saucepan over high heat. Remove from heat and add baking soda. Let it stand about 1 hour until cool.

WHISK flour and next 6 ingredients in a large bowl until blended. Whisk eggs and both sugars in another bowl until blended. Whisk oil into eggs and sugar, then whisk in cooled stout mixture. Gradually whisk liquid mixture into dry mixture. Stir in fresh ginger.

DIVIDE mixture evenly between the 3 cake pans and level tops.

BAKE until tester inserted into center of cakes comes out clean, about 25 minutes. Cool cakes in pans for 15 minutes, then invert onto cooling racks and allow to cool completely. *(Cakes can be made 1 day ahead of serving, wrapped securely. Or wrap tightly in plastic wrap, then put into plastic zip-lock bags and cool until ready to use.)*

Cream Cheese Frosting

16	ounces cream cheese, at room temperature
1	stick unsalted butter, at room temperature
¾	teaspoon finely grated orange zest
2	cups powdered sugar

BEAT cream cheese, butter, and orange zest in a large bowl until fluffy. Gradually beat in powdered sugar. Chill 30 minutes before frosting cake. Decorate with candied ginger arranged in a circle at top edge of cake.

COOK'S NOTE: Add water if frosting is too stiff to spread on cake.

Spices, Sauces & Marinades

Bouquet Garni
Hot Chili Powder
Mild Chili Powder
Chris's Hot Sauce
Dry Barbecue Rub
Garam Masala Spice Mixture
Dry Blackened Seasoning Mix
Herbes de Provence
Dry Rub for Turkey
Jerk Seasoning
Indian Style Dry Rub for Turkey
Pork Dry Rub
Rich Smoked Turkey Stock
Salsa Seasoning
Smoky Pizza Sauce
Stir-Fry Marinade
South of the (Canadian) Border Marinade
Tofu Tropical Teriyaki Marinade
Tofu Marinade

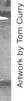

Bouquet Garni

*I vary this combination of spices according to the food
I am making. This is the one I use most often.*

1 Turkish bay leaf
3 fresh thyme sprigs
2 fresh parsley sprigs
8 black peppercorns
¼ teaspoon fennel seeds, slightly crushed

COMBINE ingredients in a cheese cloth and tie with string before immersing in the recipe.

Hot Chili Powder

3 tablespoons sweet Ancho chili pepper
3 tablespoons cayenne chili powder
1 tablespoon crushed red pepper flakes
1 tablespoon roasted, ground cumin
1 tablespoon garlic powder
1 tablespoon Mexican oregano

GRIND all ingredients together in spice or coffee grinder. Store in glass jar.

COOK'S NOTE: I use a coffee grinder often for mixing spices, but use a separate one for coffee as even a good cleaning can't prevent the residual coffee aroma from overwhelming the subtle spice flavors.

Mild Chili Powder

3   tablespoons paprika
1   tablespoon ground cumin
2   tablespoons dried oregano
1   teaspoon cayenne pepper
½   teaspoon garlic powder

GRIND all ingredients together in spice or coffee grinder. Store in glass jar.

Chris's Hot Sauce

My brother loves heat in his food. This met his approval!
It has a lingering heat that adds to almost any dish.

1 ½   cups carrots, chopped
1   yellow onion, chopped
1 ½   cups white vinegar
¼   cup lime juice
10   garlic cloves, chopped
1   teaspoon salt
1   teaspoon sugar
12   fresh habanero peppers, chopped

COMBINE all ingredients except habanero peppers in saucepan.

BOIL 19 minutes or until carrots are soft. Add habanero peppers.

PUREE in blender until smooth.

POUR in sterilized jars and refrigerate.

COOK'S NOTE: I follow regular canning instructions for a longer shelf life.

Dry Barbecue Rub

4 tablespoons sweet paprika
2 tablespoons chili powder
2 tablespoons ground cumin
2 tablespoons dark brown sugar
2 tablespoons kosher salt
1 tablespoon dried oregano
1 tablespoon granulated sugar
1 tablespoon ground black pepper
1 tablespoon ground white pepper
2 teaspoons cayenne pepper

184

MIX all ingredients together in a small bowl. (*The rub can be stored in an airtight container at room temperature for several weeks.*) Good for pork, goat, chicken or turkey.

Garam Masala Spice Mixture

1 tablespoon cardamon seeds
1 teaspoon whole cloves
1 teaspoon black peppercorns
1 teaspoon whole black cumin seeds
½ teaspoon nutmeg
¼ teaspoon mace

GRIND all ingredients together in spice or coffee grinder. Store in glass jar.

Dry Blackened Seasoning Mix

1 tablespoon Smoked Spanish Paprika, Hot*
1 tablespoon kosher salt
1 teaspoon onion powder
1 teaspoon garlic powder
1 teaspoon freshly ground peppercorns
½ teaspoon cayenne peppers
½ teaspoon ground cardamon seeds
½ teaspoon oregano
½ teaspoon thyme
1 teaspoon ancho chili powder

GRIND all ingredients together in spice or coffee grinder.
Store in glass jar. Great rub for halibut, swordfish and chicken.

* *Available from The Spice House, see Resources.*

Herbes de Provence

1 tablespoon dried basil
1 tablespoon marjoram
1 tablespoon summer savory
1 tablespoon thyme
1 crushed bay leaf
1 teaspoon lavender
1 teaspoon fennel

MIX together and store in glass container.

Dry Rub for Turkey

1 ½   tablespoons ground cardamon
1 ½   tablespoons ground ginger
1 ½   tablespoons ground black pepper
1   tablespoon ground turmeric
1   tablespoon ground roasted cumin
1   tablespoon ground coriander
1   teaspoon ground allspice
½   teaspoon ground cloves

COMBINE all ingredients together and store in glass jar.

GENTLY lift breast skin up from turkey. Rub spices on breasts and place skin back over turkey breast. Secure breast skin with 2 toothpicks. Bake or smoke, according to directions.

186

Jerk Seasoning

¼   cup crushed pineapple
6   scallions, chopped
4   garlic cloves, minced
2   tablespoons Chris's Hot Sauce *(recipe p. 183)*
1   tablespoon dark brown sugar
1   teaspoon kosher salt
1   teaspoon cinnamon
1   teaspoon ground allspice
1   teaspoon narrow-leaf French thyme

FOOD PROCESS until it resembles a paste. Great on chicken, pork and goat.

Indian Style Dry Rub for Turkey

1 ½   tablespoons ground cardamon
1 ½   tablespoons powdered ginger
1 ½   tablespoons ground black pepper
1   tablespoon ground turmeric
1   tablespoon ground roasted cumin
1   tablespoon ground coriander
1   teaspoon ground allspice
½   teaspoon ground cloves

COMBINE all ingredients together and store in glass jar.

GENTLY lift breast skin up from turkey. Rub spices on breasts and place skin back over turkey breast. Secure breast skin with 2 toothpicks. Bake or smoke, according to directions.

COOK'S NOTE: I also like to slightly salt the turkey cavity and rub spice on the inside if I am not doing a stuffing.

Pork Dry Rub

¼ cup Hungarian sweet paprika
¼ cup Smoked Spanish Paprika, Hot *(The Spice House)*
¼ cup brown sugar
3 teaspoons roasted, ground cumin
3 teaspoons Ancho chile powder
3 teaspoons black pepper
1 teaspoon cayenne
1 teaspoon ground chipotle chile pepper
3 teaspoons granulated onion
3 teaspoons granulated garlic
3 teaspoons celery seed
1 teaspoon dried oregano

GRIND all ingredients together in spice or coffee grinder. Store in glass jar.

NOTE: When preparing meat, use very liberally on both sides. Let it sit about 5 minutes, then cook or grill as you choose. Great for goat, pork, chicken or turkey.

Rich Smoked Turkey Stock

1 smoked turkey carcass, reserve turkey meat for soup
1 carrot
1 yellow onion
1 teaspoon celery seed

3   tablespoons Tortollan herbed pepper*
1   teaspoon liquid smoke
    (if carcass is not real smoky)
6   cups chicken stock
6   cups water
1   bottle white wine *(Chardonnay)*

FILL large stock pot with all ingredients. Bring to boil for 30 minutes, simmer for 6 hours.

LET STAND overnight in refrigerator. Remove top layer of fat in the morning. Simmer for 2 more hours. Drain stock into another pot for immediate use, or pour into containers for freezing for another time.

* *Available from Sunny Caribbee Spice Co. Ltd., see Resources.*

Salsa Seasoning

2   tablespoons sugar
2   tablespoons Ancho chili pepper powder
1   tablespoon garlic powder
1   tablespoon onion powder
1   tablespoon roasted, ground cumin
1   tablespoon mulatto chili pepper, ground
1   small, dried habanero *(optional for heat)*

GRIND all ingredients separately before combining together. Store in glass container.

COOK'S NOTE: To adjust heat on this fresh seasoning, start by omitting habanero and add ¼ piece at a time, test, and repeat until you reach your desired heat level.

Smoky Pizza Sauce

The liquid smoke in this sauce creates such concentration of flavor as it melds with the tomatoes; I feel it is the yummiest pizza sauce I've ever made.

5	pounds fresh, ripe tomatoes
⅓	cup olive oil
2	cups yellow onions, chopped
6	garlic cloves, minced
1	tablespoon dried sweet basil
1	teaspoon dried oregano
1	teaspoon dried narrow-leaf French thyme
½	teaspoon dried red pepper flakes
½	teaspoon liquid smoke
⅔	cup dry red wine *(Rhone like)*
1	teaspoon sea salt

190

HEAT olive oil, and then add onions and sauté for 1 minute. Add garlic, basil, thyme, oregano, and pepper flakes and heat for 15 minutes.

SQUEEZE out seeds of tomatoes and coarsely chop. Add tomatoes, liquid smoke, wine and salt. Bring to a boil then reduce to medium low and simmer for 1 hour, reduced by one-third. Cool and puree. *Can refrigerate for up to 3 days or freeze for 3 months.*

Stir-Fry Marinade

    4   tablespoons soy sauce
    3   tablespoons sherry
    3   tablespoons five-spice powder
    2   tablespoons honey
    3   garlic cloves, minced
    1   teaspoon white pepper
    ½   cup vegetable stock
    1   tablespoon corn starch

WHISK all ingredients together except corn starch. Marinate chicken or meat for 4 hours or overnight.

DRAIN, save marinade. Add corn starch to marinade and mix in with meat and vegetables during last 3 minutes of cooking.

South of the (Canadian) Border Marinade

This sauce has enough heat to keep you warm from the inside out when shoveling out from those winter storms in "the county!"

2	smoky chili peppers
1	mild chili pepper
¼	teaspoon red pepper flakes
¼	teaspoon orange zest
¼	teaspoon salt
1	cup apple cider vinegar
1	cup water
¼	cup olive oil
¼	cup pineapple juice
¼	cup lime juice

COMBINE all dry ingredients in food processor and pulse until finely chopped. Mix liquid ingredients in a bowl, add dry mixture. Marinate fish, poultry or meat for at least 1 hour before grilling. Great dip for cornbread sticks.

Tofu Tropical Teriyaki Marinade

¾ cup soy sauce
1 cup corn syrup
½ cup molasses
½ cup pineapple juice
4 garlic cloves, minced
¼ cup crushed pineapple, drained
1 package of firm tofu, cut in bite size chunks

COMBINE and pour over tofu chunks. Marinate for 3 hours, turning chunks hourly. Bake at 375°F for 15 minutes on each side. *Can refrigerate marinade for 2 days.*

Tofu Marinade

½ cup soy sauce
½ cup sherry
⅓ cup peanut oil
¼ cup orange juice
1 tablespoon sherry vinegar
5 garlic cloves, minced
1 tablespoon ginger, minced
1 tablespoon brown sugar

COMBINE all ingredients in jar. Shake vigorously. Marinate tofu for 4 hours, turning every hour, before baking or frying.

It's Five
O'Clock
Somewhere

Cold River Blueberry Cordial

Homemade Irish Cream   **195**

Indian Spiced (Chai) Tea

Katie Cooler

Maine Maple Egg Nog

Mexican MojitA

Ms. Scarlett O'Hara

Solstice Mocha

Strawberry Solstice Cordial

Spottesbrooke wine cellar

Cold River Blueberry Cordial

We all have reasons why we cease to eat or drink something anymore. My nemesis was vodka, due to a "youthful indiscretion." However, the flavor of Cold River Vodka adds such a depth of character, a sense of terroire… you'll see what brought me back.

4   cups fresh Maine blueberries
2   cups Cold River Vodka *(best flavor with this vodka)*
2   cups granulated sugar
½   teaspoon whole cloves
½   teaspoon coriander seeds
⅓   cup fresh squeezed lemon juice

PUREE blueberries in food processor. Then add all ingredients in a glass jar, shake to combine and let set in a cool place for 5 months.

COOK'S NOTE: 1) if your glass jar has a metal cover, place a thick food storage bag on the jar before you put the cover on, so the metal will not erode or transfer its taste to the cordial. 2) I make this during blueberry picking season and let it sit in our wine cellar until our Winter Solstice Party. I like the softness and depth of the flavor after it sits for 5 months. The flavor is still good after sitting for shorter periods of time. You test it!

Homemade Irish Cream

Remember the days in college when you couldn't afford the good stuff? I made my own.

- 1 cup whiskey
- 4 eggs
- 1 14-ounce can sweetened condensed milk
- 2 tablespoons Hershey's® syrup
- 2 teaspoons vanilla extract
- 1 teaspoon coconut extract

PLACE all ingredients in blender, blend on high until thoroughly combined. Set overnight in refrigerator.

COOK'S NOTE: *Good for 1 month only in the refrigerator, because of the fresh eggs.*

Indian Spiced (Chai) Tea

This is one of my favorite teas. Play with these spices to suit your taste buds.

- 4 teabags black Indian tea
- 3 teaspoons raw sugar
- 2 teaspoons honey
- 6 slices fresh ginger (or 1 teaspoon ground ginger)
- 3 whole cloves
- 6 whole green cardamon pods, broken open
- ⅛ teaspoon Vietnamese Cassia "Saigon" Cinnamon, ground fine *(from The Spice House)* dash freshly ground Tellicherry black pepper
- ½ teaspoon vanilla extract
- 5 cups water
- 2 cups whole milk *(I use non-fat vanilla soy)*

COMBINE tea and spices with water. Bring mixture to a boil. Boil 1 minute. Add milk and return to a boil. Strain and enjoy. *Serves 6*

Katie Cooler

This drink is for all those who knew me and my drink specialty list at Ruby Begonias!

- 1 ounce amaretto
- 1 ounce vodka
- 1 ounce Southern Comfort

5 ounces pineapple juice
  splash of grenadine
  splash of orgeat*

COMBINE all ingredients in a 16 ounce glass with ice. Shake and serve with pineapple chunk.

*COOK'S NOTE: Orgeat is an extract combination of almond and orange. It enhances the flavor of this drink, not that it needs it!

Maine Maple Egg Nog

This is such a wonderful winter indulgence.

½ cup Maine maple syrup
3 large eggs, well beaten
2 cups whole milk
⅛ teaspoon powdered ginger
⅓ cup Mount Gay rum
½ cup whipping cream, whipped

COMBINE maple syrup, eggs, milk and ginger; beat until combined. Add rum and pour into 4 glasses. Top with whipped cream.

COOK'S NOTE: To warm, add combined ingredients (except rum and whipped cream) to pan and simmer until heated. Pour rum into mugs and add warm milk combination, top with whipped cream.

Mexican MojitA

Don and I were in Miami and discovered a great Cuban restaurant. They blend their Mojotos and strain before serving. Here's my take, with the wonderful spirit of tequila!

30	fresh spearmint leaves
10	ice cubes
3	tablespoons raw brown sugar, ground separately
⅓	cup fresh squeezed lime juice
3	ounces tequila *(I like Patron Silver)*
1¼	ounces orange liqueur *(I like Patron Citronge)*
¼	cup club soda

200

LAYER the spearmint, ice, ground sugar, lime juice, tequila, and orange liquer in a blender. Blend on high until pulverized, about 15 seconds. Strain through a fine sieve.

LIME the edge of two margarita glasses. Pour in club soda and top with strained mixture. Serve with lime wedge. *Makes 2 large drinks.*

Ms. Scarlett O'Hara

Here is an old time favorite of mine in the winter.

1½	ounces Southern Comfort
1	teaspoon fresh lime juice
4	ounces cranberry juice
	splash of club soda
	lime wedge

FILL A ROCKS GLASS half full with ice. Pour Southern Comfort, lime juice, and cranberry juice over ice. Lime the edge of the glass and put lime into the drink, top with a splash of club soda.

Solstice Mocha

So many Solstice traditions!

1   quart half and half
1   cup strong coffee
¼   cup Mount Gay rum
¼   cup maple syrup
2   teaspoons vanilla
    cinnamon and nutmeg

HEAT in saucepan half and half, coffee and maple syrup. Add rum and vanilla and pour into mugs. Top with nutmeg and cinnamon.

Strawberry Solstice Cordial

I have been making this cordial since 1991. Each year I buy the strawberries around the 4th of July, and the cordial sits until the Winter Solstice Party.

1   gallon strawberries, hulled and halved
5   cups sugar
1   quart French brandy

PUT half the strawberries in a glass gallon jar. Add 2 cups of sugar. Fill the jar with the rest of the strawberries and add remaining sugar and brandy. Place a quart size freezer bag over jar opening and then the cover on top. Shake vigorously until sugar is dissolved. Place in a cool, dark area until the holidays. Drain through a cheese cloth and pour into bottles.

COOK'S NOTE: It's worth the six month wait. This is a great holiday gift.

Things To Do In Maine

From antiquing, art galleries, lighthouses, museums, and theatres to fall foliage, hiking, skiing, music, whale watching and so much more. Check the local Chamber of Commerce web sites for more information.

Artwork by Judy Taylor

Winter Season / JANUARY-FEBRUARY

**INTERNATIONAL ICE-CARVING COMPETITION
AND WINTER CARNIVAL** – Freeport/Falmouth (Jan)

OXFORD HILLS SNOWFEST – Norway (Jan)

SNOW MOUNTAIN BIKE RACE – Bridgton (Jan)

**JEEP KING OF THE MOUNTAIN PROFESSIONAL
SKIING AND SNOWBOARDING WORLD CHAMPIONSHIPS**
– Sunday River/Newry (Feb)

KATAHDIN AREA WINTERFEST – Millinocket (Feb)

**MAINE DERBY FEST / TOTALLY INSANE
ICE FISHING FESTIVAL** – Raymond (Feb)

MUSHERS BOWL – Fryeburg (Feb)

PLUM CREEK 100-MILE WILDERNESS SLED DOG RACE
– Greenville (Feb)

**TELEMARK FESTIVAL AT SUNDAY RIVER
SKI RESORT** – Newry (Feb)

US NATIONAL TOBOGGAN CHAMPIONSHIPS
– Camden (Feb) *Watch for the Black Fly Stew Team in 2008!*

Mud Season / MARCH-JUNE

JACKMAN MAINE SLED DOG SPRINT RACE
– Moose River (Mar)

ROCK MAPLE SNOWCROSS SNOWMOBILE RACING
– Skowhegan (Mar)

BOOTHBAY HARBOR ANNUAL FISHERMAN'S FESTIVAL
– Boothbay Harbor (April)

SUGARLOAF ANNUAL REGGAE SKI FESTIVAL
– Rangeley (April)

MOOSE MAINEA FESTIVAL – Greenville (May-June)

Black Fly Season / JUNE-AUGUST

BOOTHBAY HARBOR MAINE'S WINDJAMMER DAYS FESTIVAL
– Boothbay Harbor (June)

OLD PORT FESTIVAL – Portland (June)

STRAWBERRY FESTIVAL – South Berwick (June)

BATH HERITAGE DAYS – Bath (June-July)

BOWDOIN SUMMER MUSIC FESTIVAL
– Bowden (June-August)

Tourist Season / JULY-SEPTEMBER

BAR HARBOR MUSIC FESTIVAL – Bar Harbor (July)

MAINE'S NORTH ATLANTIC BLUES FESTIVAL
– Rockland (July)

YARMOUTH CLAM FESTIVAL – Yarmouth (July)

OLD ORCHARD BEACH MAINE ANNUAL SANDCASTLE CONTEST
– Old Orchard Beach (July)

PORTLAND CHAMBER MUSIC FESTIVAL
– Portland (Aug)

SALTWATER MUSIC FESTIVAL – Brunswick (Aug)

MAINE ANTIQUES FESTIVAL – Union (August)

HIGHLAND GAMES FESTIVAL – Brunswick (August)

MAINE LOBSTER FESTIVAL – Rockland (August)

MS REGATTA HARBORFEST WEEKEND – Portland (August)

GREAT FALLS BALLOON FESTIVAL
– Lewiston/Auburn (August)

THOMAS POINT BEACH BLUEGRASS FESTIVAL
– Brunswick (Sept)

COMMON GROUND FAIR – Unity (Sept)

CAPRICCIO FESTIVAL OF THE ARTS
– Ogunquit (September)

Winter Season / OCTOBER-DECEMBER

WIFE CARRYING CONTEST AND COLUMBUS DAY FESTIVAL AT SUNDAY RIVER – Newry (Oct)

YORK VILLAGE FESTIVAL OF LIGHTS – York (Dec)

OGUNQUIT MAINE'S ANNUAL CHRISTMAS BY THE SEA FESTIVAL – Ogunquit (Dec)

KENNEBUNKPORT MAINE'S CHRISTMAS PRELUDE CELEBRATION – Kennebunkport (Dec)

Lupines by Kate Gooding

Resources

This cookbook was created with the help of many hands, none more creative than the Purveyors of specialty foods whose personal pride in their products is an inspiration to cooks everywhere, and the Artists whose works I am proud to display alongside my recipes.

PURVEYORS

BAR HARBOR BREWING CO.

Todd & Suzanne M. Foster
135 Otter Creek Drive
Bar Harbor, ME 04609
(207)288-4592
www.barharborbrewing.com
best brewed beer!

BAR HARBOR CELLARS

Matt Gerald / Petko Ivanof
Route 3
Bar Harbor, ME 04609
(207) 288-3907
www.barharborcellars.com
Delicious wines for anytime

COLD RIVER VODKA

Bob Hawkins
US Route 1
Freeport, ME
(207) 865-4828
www.coldrivervodka.com
great vodka from Maine potatoes

DOWNEAST LOBSTER COMPANY

Ron Doane
1192 Bar Harbor Road
Trenton, ME 04605
(207) 667-8589
great local seafood

MAINE GOODIES

George and Terri Stone
PO Box 288
Albion, Maine 04910
(207) 437-2052
Toll Free: (866) 385-6238
www.mainegoodies.com
selection of Maine products

MAINE GUIDE SERVICES

Chris Krukowski
86 Pleasant Street
Moose River, ME 04945
(207) 668-5041
moose, deer, birds, fish and black flies

MDI SHELLFISH COMPANY

David Smith
118 Bass Harbor Road
Southwest Harbor, ME 04679
(207) 244-7048
fresh crabmeat

MINERAL SPRINGS MUSHROOMS

Andrew Smith
Newport, ME
(207) 322-8138
organically grown mushrooms

PURVEYORS

PECTIC SEAFOOD

Paul & Teresa Cecere
153 Hall Quarry Road
Mount Desert, ME 04660
(207) 244-7544 or (800) 860-3979
www.pecticseafood.com
fresh seafood and so much more

SAWYER'S SPECIALTIES

Scott Worcester
Route 102, Main St
Southwest Harbor, ME 04679
(207) 244-3317
scott_worcester@yahoo.com
many of our wines come from their great selection

SUNNY CARIBBEE SPICE CO. LTD

119 Main Street
Road Town, Tortola, BVI
Tel. (284) 494-2178   Fax (284) 494-4039
sunnycaribbee@surfbvi.com
www.SunnyCaribbee.com
Tortollan Pepper

SUNSET ACRES FARM & DAIRY

Bob Bowen and Anne Bossi
769 Bagaduce Road
Brooksville, Maine 04617
207-326-4741, 207-326-0861
www.sunsetacresfarm.com
incredible goat cheese products

SWEET ENERGY
Tim Ziter
195 Acorn Lane
Colchester, VT 05446
(802) 655-1372
www.sweetenergy.com
goji berries, dried fruit, nuts, chocolate and more

TATE'S STRAWBERRIES
Albert Tate
Route 43
Cornish, ME
(207) 285-3410
seasonal fresh strawberries

THE SPICE HOUSE
Patty Penzy Erd
1512 North Wells Street
Chicago, IL 60610
(312) 274 0378
www.thespicehouse.com
I buy almost all the spices and herbs that I don't grow from Patty

ARTWORK

R. SCOTT BALTZ STUDIO
PO Box 671, 188 Pretty Marsh Road
Mount Desert, ME 04660
(207) 244-5792
scott@rscottbaltz.com
www.rscottbaltz.com
p. 89

GAIL CLEVELAND/
SMART STUDIO
PO Box 413, Main Street
Northeast Harbor, ME 04662
(207) 276-5152
gailc@smart-studio.com
www.smart-studio.com
p. 43

TOM CURRY STUDIO
PO Box 65
Brooklin, ME 04616
(207) 359-9880
tcurry@tomcurrymaineartist.com
www.tomcurrymaineartist.com
p. 181

RUSSELL D'ALESSIO/
PRETTY MARSH GALLERY
15 Cottage Street
Bar Harbor, ME 04609
(207) 288-9442
russ@rdalessio.com
www.rdalessio.com
cover art, contents, p. 1, p. 63, p. 69

MARION SMITH STUDIO
30 Atlantic Ave.
Bar Harbor, ME 04609
(207) 288-4014
marionsm@acadia.net
p. 149

JUDY TAYLOR STUDIO AND GALLERY
363 Main St.
Southwest Harbor, ME 04679
(207) 244-5545
punchinellas@hotmail.com
www.judytaylorstudio.com
p. 29, p. 202

Attean Lookout, my favorite view in the U.S.!

D

E

Egg Nog, Maine Maple, 199
Eggplant
    Caviar, 8
    Garam Masala, 45

F

Fettuccini
    Seafood, 85
    with Braised Rabbit, 120
Fiddleheads, Steamed, 44
Fish *see also* Seafood
    Char Provençal, 76
    Halibut, Grilled, 80
    Salmon
        Cedar Smoked, 75
        Hot and Sweet Grilled, 80
        Peppered Jerky, 84
        Smoked, Cheese Ball, 13
    Sole, Asian Lobster Stuffed, 68
    Swordfish, Grilled, with Mango
        Salsa, 83
Foccacia, Whole Wheat and Rosemary, 21
Frosting, Cream Cheese, 158, 179
Fudge, Goat's Milk Peanut Butter, 157

G

Game
    Bear
        Bourguignon, 90
        Casserole, 91
        Roasted Cumin Rubbed, and
            Cabernet Glaze, 92
        Stew, 94
    Beaver
        Baked Beans, 95
        Chili, 96

INDEX

226